U.S. Department of Justice
Office of Justice Programs
National Institute of Justice

NIJ

'05

NATIONAL INSTITUTE OF JUSTICE

Annual Report

To the President, the Attorney General, and the Congress:

It is my honor to transmit the National Institute of Justice's annual report on research, development, and evaluation for fiscal year 2005, pursuant to Title 1 of the Omnibus Crime Control and Safe Streets Act of 1968.

Respectfully submitted,

Glenn R. Schmitt
Acting Director, National Institute of Justice
Washington, D.C.

Annual Report

NATIONAL INSTITUTE OF JUSTICE

U.S. Department of Justice
Office of Justice Programs

810 Seventh Street, N.W.
Washington, DC 20531

Alberto R. Gonzales
Attorney General

Regina B. Schofield
Assistant Attorney General

Glenn R. Schmitt
Acting Director, National Institute of Justice

This and other publications and products of the
National Institute of Justice can be found at:

National Institute of Justice
www.ojp.usdoj.gov/nij

Office of Justice Programs
Partnerships for Safer Communities
www.ojp.usdoj.gov

Table of Contents

Highlights of the Year

The criminal justice professional faces new challenges every day. Tremendous changes are taking place in law enforcement, crime prevention, and intervention strategies. Across all disciplines, the field is adapting to new threats from transnational, electronic, and terrorist criminal activity. These threats have augmented, not replaced, more traditional crimes.

At the same time, breakthroughs in technology research and development, most notably involving DNA analysis, biometrics, and less-lethal technologies, are altering law enforcement priorities and operations. Complementary social science research is assessing the impacts of technological change. Researchers are using methods such as crime mapping and information analysis to uncover crime patterns and design interventions tailored to address local problems—In collaboration with Federal, State, and local authorities.

But breakthroughs have impact only to the degree they are applied. The National Institute of Justice (NIJ) helps criminal justice professionals discover and apply research and development breakthroughs to real-life situations—in the community, the courtroom, correctional institutions, and even on the Internet.

What is NIJ?

NIJ was created in 1968 by the Omnibus Crime Control and Safe Streets Act, 42 USC §§3721–3723. Its budget has grown from $2.4 million to almost $300 million, funding the oversight of more than 500 grants each year (see appendix A). NIJ is the Nation's primary resource for advancing scientific research, development, and evaluation to enhance the administration of justice and public safety. These efforts are geared toward helping criminal justice practitioners understand, apply, and benefit from new tools, technologies, and research findings. NIJ tackles research and technology challenges that State and local agencies are not equipped to address, crafting solutions that are comprehensive in scope while useful to practitioners. Many recent advances in law enforcement tools and technology were supported by NIJ-funded research.

As never before, today's criminal justice practitioner needs access to the most up-to-date tools and information to be effective.

In effect, NIJ acts as the Nation's objective third party on issues of crime and justice. Congress, criminal justice agencies, industry, and the public all look to NIJ for answers to questions of national and international importance, such as: How can State and local agencies expand their DNA analysis capabilities? What are the best methods for identifying missing persons? What body armor best protects police officers? How can information on terrorist activities be collected and analyzed? Why do so many prisoners recidivate? What are the characteristics of identity theft criminals? Do batterer intervention programs work?

Criminal justice agencies count on NIJ to develop needed research knowledge, tools, and technologies and to establish and maintain performance-based standards against which they can be tested. Practitioners rely on NIJ to make these research-based resources accessible. For example, the State of Louisiana used a prepublication version of an NIJ-funded report on forensic examination of degraded remains to help identify the missing after Hurricane Katrina.[1]

NIJ's overarching goal is to improve real-world operations and results. Grantees are selected through open, national competition and rigorous independent peer review.[2] Fiscal year 2005 (FY 2005) grants and grantees are listed in appendix B.

Challenges

In 2004, violent crime reached an 11-year low, with 5.2 million violent crimes reported. Property crimes have stabilized since 2002 at 77 percent of reported crimes. Statistics do not tell the full story, however. Some jurisdictions continue to experience high crime rates. Despite gains in reducing juvenile gun violence in some cities, criminal activity that used to be relatively rare—such as identity theft fraud and transnational gang violence—is encroaching upon average Americans. Offenders are increasingly mobile, crossing State and even international borders. Homicide clearance rates are declining—one-third of homicides each year are not cleared through arrests.[3] Local agencies must grapple with emerging threats as diverse as methamphetamine use, Internet predators, human trafficking, and terrorism.

[1] The Kinship and Data Analysis Panel (KADAP) report is discussed in chapter 2.

[2] A description of the grant process and current and past solicitations are on the Web at www.ojp.usdoj.gov/nij/funding.htm.

[3] Index violent crime offenses on the Federal Bureau of Investigation's Uniform Crime Reports (UCR) are murder, forcible rape, robbery, and aggravated assault. UCR Index property crime offenses are burglary, larceny-theft, and motor vehicle theft. Crime statistics are from the Bureau of Justice Statistics Web site at www.ojp.usdoj.gov/bjs/cvict.htm.

Law enforcement must become increasingly agile to counter these threats, which requires seamless collaboration and communication among Federal, State, and local law enforcement and other first responders. As never before, today's criminal justice practitioner needs access to the most up-to-date tools and information to be effective.

Working for results

Research and development supported by NIJ is geared toward getting results that directly assist State and local practitioners and policymakers in today's dynamic environment. Progress cannot take place in a vacuum; input from the field, practitioner-researcher partnerships, and enduring collaborations ensure success where it counts: in local communities.

The social and physical sciences are increasingly interrelated as researchers and practitioners pursue better understanding and improved practices. NIJ-sponsored interventions built on researcher-practitioner partnerships reduced juvenile gun violence in many U.S. cities. This work continued in FY 2005 with Project Safe Neighborhoods and other collaborations.[4]

Partnerships also form the core of NIJ's technology development process. Technical working groups made up of practitioners and subject matter experts guide the agency's technology investments and evaluate its products. NIJ also regularly convenes social science researchers and practitioners to recommend where research and evaluation efforts are most needed. Thus, all of NIJ's work is based on a validated requirement brought to the agency by criminal justice practitioners.

DNA analysis and forensic databases have revolutionized crime solving. Since 2003, NIJ has provided unprecedented funding and technical assistance to State and local crime laboratories in support of the President's DNA Initiative. NIJ has also sponsored ground-breaking research that is advancing the speed and accuracy of DNA identification tools and fostering improvements in other

[4] See note 25, page 17.

At the National Strategy Meeting on Identifying the Missing, medical examiners, law enforcement officials, prosecutors, forensic scientists, key policymakers, victim advocates, and family members gathered to share experiences, develop a national strategy, and foster collaboration.

NIJ sponsored, participated in, or otherwise supported 56 meetings, conferences, and events in FY 2005. Some key events:

- *Annual Research & Evaluation Conference.*
- *Community Corrections Conference.*
- *Corrections Technology Institute.*
- *Crime Mapping Research Conference.*
- *Critical Incident Technology Conference.*
- *DNA Grantees Workshop.*
- *Innovative Technologies for Community Corrections Conference.*
- *Law Enforcement Technology Institute.*
- *Less-Lethal Technology Symposium.*
- *Longitudinal Studies Workshop.*
- *Mock Prison Riot™.*
- *National Conference on Science, Technology, and the Law.*
- *School Violence Prevention Research Workshop.*
- *Workshop on Predisposition Revictimization in Cases of Violence Against Women.*

forensic tools such as fingerprint analysis and digital evidence examination. Most evidence from crime scenes, however, does not yield a DNA profile. NIJ is sponsoring standards and training for practitioners who need to be proficient in collecting, managing, and presenting DNA evidence.

NIJ-sponsored research has yielded substantive knowledge about the nature of victimization and its consequences, especially violence against women, elder abuse, crimes against children, and pervasive victimization among isolated segments of society. Research has also focused on helping service providers, law enforcement officers, and other allied professionals who work with victims. A better understanding of the prevalence and consequences of victimization is vital as the Nation faces the global spread of terrorism, human trafficking, child exploitation, and rape.

An eventful year

Although DNA-related operational funding accounted for the largest share of expenditures in FY 2005, NIJ funded 169 grants in 22 other areas of research, development, and evaluation (see appendix B). Broadly, these areas cover:

- Developing and improving law enforcement and corrections technology, tools, and operations.
- Studying the prevalence and consequences of violence and victimization within communities and corrections.
- Understanding and preventing terrorism and transnational crimes.
- Informing practitioners, policymakers, researchers, and the public about criminal justice research findings and technological advances.

Identifying human remains is one of several key objectives of the President's DNA Initiative. In April, NIJ worked with other U.S. Department of Justice (DOJ) agencies to convene the first National Strategy Meeting on Identifying the

Missing. Medical examiners, law enforcement officials, prosecutors, forensic scientists, key policymakers, victim advocates, and family members gathered to share experiences, develop a national strategy, and foster collaboration.

Earlier in the year, NIJ and the Office on Violence Against Women sponsored a national workshop exploring the revictimization that often occurs between arrest and case disposition. Representatives from probation and police departments, shelters, and pretrial services in 14 States and Washington, DC, met with victim advocates, defense attorneys, judges, prosecutors, and researchers to discuss how to prevent revictimization and areas for future research.[5]

The Attorney General's Body Armor Safety Initiative testing program continued in FY 2005. NIJ promulgated a major revision to its 30-year-old body armor compliance program. For the first time, manufacturers must be able to demonstrate that their products meet NIJ's performance standards over the full warranty life of the armor. NIJ also issued an advisory notice to law enforcement users that Zylon® and PBO[6] may present a safety risk.

NIJ also launched an initiative concerning the use of less-lethal weapons, such as those sold under the brand name Taser®. NIJ worked closely with the International Association of Chiefs of Police to disseminate information to law enforcement agencies trying to make informed choices about the deployment of these devices.

As the fiscal year came to a close, NIJ staff were working overtime to help with the Federal Government's Katrina response. Staff provided field support and equipment such as off-road vehicles, boats, and robots requested by emergency responders; onsite support in affected areas; communications interoperability switches to allow users of disparate radios to talk to each other; and unmanned aerial vehicles for aerial photography and mapping.

[5] See www.ojp.usdoj.gov/nij/vawprog/pred_vic_summary.html for the workshop summary and a list of attendees.

[6] Poly-p-phenylene benzobisoxazole. See note 20, page 15

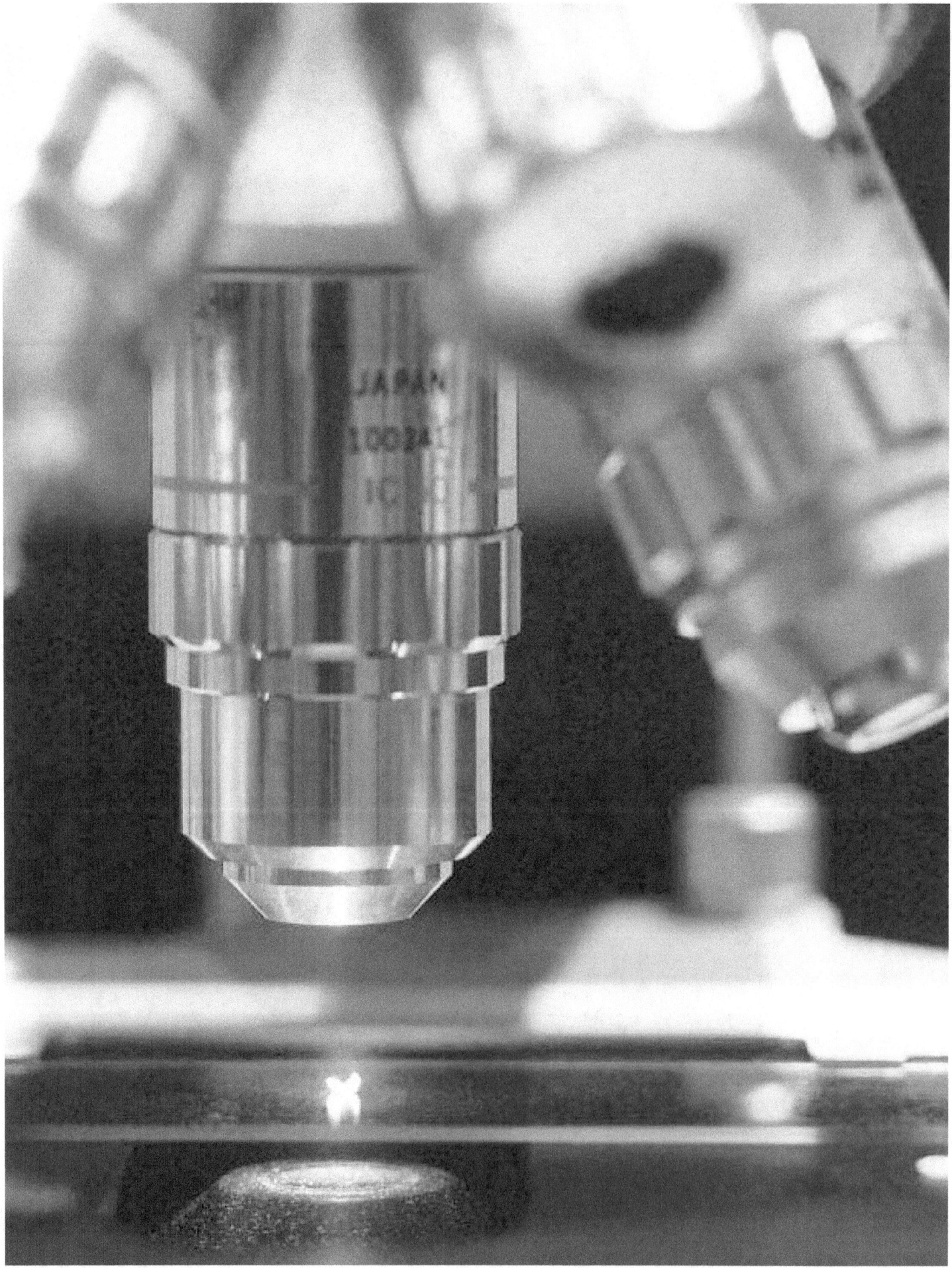

Accomplishments in Forensics

NIJ remains at the forefront of forensic science research, development, evaluation, and application. DNA applications are the most prominent of these efforts, but NIJ-funded researchers are also focusing on other disciplines, including controlled substances, friction ridge analysis (fingerprints, palmprints, and footprints), anthropology, firearms and toolmarks, toxicology, and trace evidence. NIJ is also working to ensure that criminal investigators are trained in recognizing evidence on seized computers.

The impact of NIJ's work in the field of forensics is profound, affecting police officers, prosecutors, defense attorneys, judges, corrections officials, forensic scientists, victim service providers, medical personnel, and victims' families.

Forensic DNA

DNA technology is being used extensively to solve crimes, exonerate the innocent, and identify human remains. This technique has captured the public's interest—a fascination likely to increase as more cold cases are solved, more persons wrongfully convicted are freed, and other benefits become apparent locally, nationally, and globally.

In 1988, the Federal Bureau of Investigation began using DNA analysis to solve crimes and in 1990 established the Combined DNA Index System (CODIS). The CODIS database allows Federal, State, and local crime laboratories to exchange and compare DNA profiles electronically to establish links between crimes and/or convicted offenders.[7]

In 2003, acting on behalf of President George W. Bush, Attorney General John Ashcroft announced a new national initiative, *Advancing Justice Through DNA Technology*. The Initiative included a proposal to allocate $1 billion over 5 years to develop, improve, and build capacity for Federal, State, and local use of DNA analysis to solve crime. The Initiative's overall goals are to:

- Eliminate backlogs of unanalyzed DNA samples for the most serious violent offenses—rapes, murders, and kidnappings—and for convicted offender samples that need testing.

[7] For more information, see the CODIS Web site at www.fbi.gov/hq/lab/codis/index1.htm.

The impact of NIJ's work in the field of forensics is profound, affecting police officers, prosecutors, defense attorneys, judges, corrections officials, forensic scientists, victim service providers, medical personnel, and victims' families.

- Strengthen crime laboratories' capacity to process DNA samples efficiently and cost-effectively and avoid future backlogs.

- Stimulate research and development of more efficient methods of DNA analysis and improve laboratory capability to analyze smaller and more degraded samples.

- Train the wide variety of professionals involved in using DNA evidence in the criminal justice system.

- Ensure that DNA technology is used to its full potential in solving missing persons cases and identifying human remains.

NIJ has played a central role in support of the President's DNA Initiative, awarding more than $108 million in grant funds in FY 2005 for this purpose.[8] Specific DNA-related programs[9] managed by NIJ include:

- Forensic Casework DNA Backlog Reduction Program.

- Convicted Offender DNA Backlog Reduction Program.

- DNA Capacity Enhancement Program.

- Using DNA to Identify Missing Persons.

- Forensic DNA Research and Development Program.

- DNA Training for the Criminal Justice Community.

Since 2004, NIJ has provided funding to State and local agencies to reduce casework backlogs by nearly 49,000 cases and convicted offender backlogs by more than 1.2 million samples (see exhibit 1). As of December 29, 2005, at least 3,100 matches on CODIS were reported to NIJ by agencies that received funding under NIJ's DNA Backlog Reduction Programs. During this same period, NIJ also awarded nearly $68 million to 211 State and local agencies to build or enhance their DNA analysis capabilities (see exhibit A-5 in appendix A).

[8] See appendix A, exhibit A-5. Appendix B lists all FY 2005 grants, grantees, and awards.

[9] For more information about these programs, see the NIJ Web site at www.ojp.usdoj.gov/nij/topics/forensics/welcome.html and the President's DNA Initiative Web site at www.DNA.gov.

Exhibit 1. Accomplishments under the President's DNA Initiative*

Program	FY 2004	FY 2005	Total
DNA Casework Backlog Reduction	29,414 cases funded	19,539 cases funded	48,953 cases
DNA Convicted Offender Backlog Reduction	474,279 samples funded	752,793 samples funded	1,294,898 samples
DNA Capacity Enhancement	106 agencies funded	105 agencies funded	211 awards

*Reported as of December 2005.

Using DNA to solve property crimes. Some police departments have found that analyzing DNA from property crimes can yield major public safety benefits because the perpetrators of these crimes are often repeat offenders who have committed, or are capable of committing, violent crimes.[10] Property crimes, particularly burglary and auto theft, often generate biological evidence from which DNA samples can be obtained. Eliminating backlogs and strengthening laboratory capacity will enable crime analysts to process more DNA samples from property crime.

On October 1, 2005, NIJ launched the DNA Expansion Demonstration Program, which will assess the contributions that DNA makes to solving high-volume serious crime and identify cost-effective practices for collecting, analyzing, and utilizing DNA evidence in such cases. The program will enable selected jurisdictions to expand DNA evidence collection beyond homicides and sexual assaults to property crimes.

Five sites have entered into 18-month interagency agreements with NIJ to implement the program: Denver, Colorado; Los Angeles, California; Orange County, California; Phoenix, Arizona; and Topeka, Kansas. All these sites have expanded DNA evidence collection to residential burglary. Some have also expanded it

[10] See Zedlewski, E., and M. Murphy, "DNA Analysis for 'Minor' Crimes: A Major Benefit for Law Enforcement," *NIJ Journal* 253 (January 2006): 2–5, available at www.ojp.usdoj.gov/nij/journals/253/dna_analysis.html.

The overarching lessons learned were that decisions made during the first 48 hours after a mass fatality shape the scope of the identification effort and that every jurisdiction should have an advance plan for identifying mass disaster victims through DNA analysis.

to commercial burglary and/or theft from auto. Investigators, forensic scientists, and representatives from the District Attorney's office are collaborating to ensure that the program is fully implemented. The Urban Institute is evaluating the program.

DNA research and development

NIJ continues to support the development of tools and technologies to assist the crime laboratory community. In FY 2005, new projects included the development of miniaturized DNA testing devices, improved tools for analyzing DNA evidence samples that are limited in quantity or degraded, and better methods for working with DNA mixtures.

Identifying the missing. Missing persons cases are painful for family and friends and difficult for investigators to solve. Recent improvements in DNA technology and the advent of nationwide DNA databases have substantially increased authorities' ability to identify remains and to resolve long-term missing persons cases. Success usually depends upon proper collection and handling of evidence; on collaboration among law enforcement, forensic scientists, medical examiners, and coroners; and on the cooperation of family members. NIJ and other DOJ agencies formed a task force to address the problems associated with identifying the missing and to foster cross-jurisdictional collaboration.

In conjunction with other DOJ agencies, NIJ sponsored the first National Strategy Meeting on Identifying the Missing in Philadelphia, Pennsylvania, on April 28–29, 2005. Participants represented many disciplines—Federal, State, and local law enforcement; coroners and medical examiners; forensic scientists; policymakers; and victim advocates—as well as surviving family members. Topics included collecting, analyzing, and identifying human remains; principles and models of collaboration; the role of the Federal Bureau of Investigation; ethical and legal issues; and the development of a comprehensive approach to identifying missing persons.[11]

[11] Conference agenda and session descriptions are available at www.DNA.gov.

Lessons learned from 9/11—The KADAP report. A few weeks after the 9/11 attacks, more than 2,000 people were still reported missing. In response, NIJ brought together a group of experts to help with the identification of victims—the most difficult job of its kind ever undertaken by the forensic community. The Kinship and DNA Analysis Panel (KADAP)—which included academics and forensic scientists from Federal and State agencies—was tasked with identifying the many challenges associated with large-scale DNA identification efforts following a mass disaster. In addition to management and infrastructure challenges, KADAP had to address the problems associated with DNA analysis of degraded samples and consider the application of novel DNA technologies and statistical approaches for this purpose.[12]

The overarching lessons learned were that decisions made during the first 48 hours after a mass fatality incident shape the scope of the identification effort and that every jurisdiction should have an advance plan for identifying mass disaster victims.

The report, *Lessons Learned From 9/11: DNA Identification in Mass Fatality Incidents,* will be released through the President's DNA Initiative in 2006 and will include a self-assessment tool to help DNA laboratories determine their level of preparedness. KADAP's influence has already been felt—the report was provided to authorities to help in the identification of victims of the South Asian tsunami and Hurricane Katrina.

For more information

- A comprehensive review of the President's DNA Initiative is at www.DNA.gov.
- NIJ has published several guides and reports on DNA.[13] Four publications were released in FY 2005:
  - *DNA in 'Minor' Crimes Yields Major Benefits in Public Safety*, November 2004, NCJ 207203, available at www.ncjrs.gov/pdffiles1/nij/207203.pdf.

[12] See *Q&A with John Butler, NIST Chemist,* National Institute of Standards and Technology, November 17, 2005, available at www.nist.gov/public_affairs/newsfromnist_DNAinterview.htm.

[13] See www.nij.ncjrs.gov/publications/pubs_db.asp and select "Advanced Search> Investigative and Forensic Sciences" for a complete list of NIJ publications on DNA forensics.

Proper presentation of digital evidence in court has become vital, as law enforcement agencies and prosecutors increase efforts to fight Internet crimes, identity theft, intellectual property crime, and cyber-terrorism.

- *Identifying Victims Using DNA: A Guide for Families,* April 2005, NCJ 209493, available at www.ncjrs.gov/pdffiles1/nij/209493.pdf (English) or www.ncjrs.gov/pdffiles1/nij/209493_spanish.pdf (Spanish).

- *Mass Fatality Incidents: A Guide for Human Forensic Identification,* Special Report, June 2005, NCJ 199758, available at www.ncjrs.gov/pdffiles1/nij/199758.pdf.

- "DNA Analysis for 'Minor' Crimes: A Major Benefit for Law Enforcement," Zedlewski, E., and M. Murphy, *NIJ Journal* 253 (January 2006): 2–5, available at www.ojp.usdoj.gov/nij/journals/253/dna_analysis.html.

Other areas of forensic science

Friction ridge analysis. In 2005, NIJ provided more than $2.5 million for research and development to increase understanding of the individuality of friction ridge patterns (fingerprints, palmprints, and footprints) and to develop and improve methods of collecting and analyzing prints. Grantees are developing software and methods to enhance the analysis and comparison of friction ridge characteristics, to better understand the growth pattern of fingerprints for identification of children, and to create tools that enable fast capture and processing of friction ridge images.

Computer forensics. Of particular concern in the era of the Internet is how to properly obtain digital evidence from crime scenes, analyze it, and present it effectively in court. To address these issues,[14] NIJ established the Electronic Crime Partnership Initiative (ECPI), comprising experts drawn from law enforcement, academia, and the private sector. ECPI helps State and local law enforcement identify, seize, and process electronic crime evidence.

Cyber-crime and cyber-terrorism are proliferating and bringing transnational organized crime into U.S. homes and communities. ECPI is focusing on a variety of electronic crimes, such as cyber weapons, Internet crimes against children, and electronic fraud, and identifying ways to fight digital crime effectively. Six working groups are building collaborative networks among and developing procedures for Federal, State, and local agencies; industry; and academia.[15]

[14] These needs were articulated in Stambaugh, H., D.S. Beaupre, D.J. Icove, R. Baker, W. Cassaday, and W.P. Williams, *Electronic Crime Needs Assessment for State and Local Law Enforcement,* March 2001, NCJ 186276, available at www.ncjrs.gov/pdffiles1/nij/186276.pdf.

[15] See www.ojp.usdoj.gov/nij/topics/ecrime/ecpi.htm for details.

Fast Capture Fingerprints Initiative

NIJ grantees are developing technologies that will capture fingerprint images in 15 seconds or less and palms in 1 minute or less. The goal is to develop a device to scan fingers and palms for expedited processing of inmates, border security checks, background checks, and other uses. This capability will improve officer safety, eliminate misidentification of subjects, and reduce costs.

NIJ is working with the Federal Bureau of Investigation, the U.S. Department of Homeland Security, the U.S. Department of State, and other agencies on this and a number of biometrics projects (see page 22) and is a cosponsor of the Biometrics Catalog at www.biometricscatalog. org/Introduction/default.aspx.

NIJ has also partnered with the National Institute of Standards and Technology and other Federal, State, and local agencies to develop a program to test computer forensic software tools. Test results help users make informed choices about acquiring and using these tools.[16] NIJ also funds the National Software Reference Library, a compilation of the digital signatures of known software applications.[17]

Proper presentation of digital evidence in court has become vital, as law enforcement agencies and prosecutors fight Internet crimes, identity theft,[18] intellectual property crime, and cyber-terrorism. NIJ technical working groups composed of governmental and industry experts are developing detailed, user-friendly guides for criminal justice professionals. Two guides are currently under development: *Investigations Involving the Internet and Computer Networks* and *Digital Evidence in the Courtroom.*

For more information

- *Test Results for Software Write Block Tools: PDBLOCK Version 1.02 (PDB_LITE)*, June 2005, NCJ 209831, available at www.ojp.usdoj.gov/nij/pubs-sum/209831.htm.

- NIJ's Electronic Crime Research and Development Web page: www.ojp.usdoj.gov/nij/topics/ecrime/welcome.html.

- *Electronic Crime Scene Investigation: A Guide for First Responders*, Special Report, July 2001, NCJ 187736, available at www.ncjrs.gov/pdffiles1/nij/187736.pdf.

- *Forensic Examination of Digital Evidence: A Guide for Law Enforcement*, Special Report, April 2004, NCJ 199408, available at www.ncjrs.gov/pdffiles1/nij/199408.pdf.

- *Status and Needs of Forensic Science Service Providers: A Report to Congress*, March 2006, NCJ 213420, available at www.ojp.usdoj.gov/nij/pubs-sum/213420.htm.

- "Without a Trace? Advances in Detecting Trace Evidence," *NIJ Journal* 249 (July 2003), available at www.ncjrs.gov/pdffiles1/jr000249b.pdf.

[16] Test results are available at www.cftt.nist.gov.

[17] See www.nsrl.nist.gov.

[18] NIJ's identity theft initiatives are discussed in chapter 3.

Policing and Corrections

In carrying out its mandate to help Federal, State, and local agencies in the fight against crime, NIJ is committed to research and development that yields results, and to identifying what works for practitioners.

Police safety

Body armor. On November 18, 2003, Attorney General John Ashcroft announced the DOJ's Body Armor Safety Initiative in response to concerns from the law enforcement community about the effectiveness of body armor then in use.[19] These concerns followed the failure of a relatively new Zylon®-based[20] body armor vest worn by a Forest Hills, Pennsylvania, police officer. The Attorney General directed NIJ to undertake an examination of Zylon®-based bullet-resistant armor (both new and used), to analyze upgrade kits provided by manufacturers that retrofit Zylon®-based bullet-resistant armors, and to review the existing program by which bullet-resistant armor is tested to determine whether the process needed modification. As part of the Body Armor Safety Initiative, NIJ issued three status reports to the Attorney General containing results from the body armor studies.[21]

In August 2005, NIJ issued *NIJ 2005 Interim Requirements for Bullet-Resistant Body Armor.* These requirements reflect a fundamental revision in how body armor is tested—the performance of body armor will now be evaluated throughout its service life, rather than only when the armor is new. The new requirements were promulgated on an interim basis to address recent NIJ research findings indicating that certain body armor models previously found to be compliant with earlier NIJ requirements for ballistic resistance of new body armor (including NIJ Standard 0101.04) may not adequately maintain ballistic performance during their service life. NIJ recommends the selection of body armor models that comply with the 2005 interim requirements.[22]

[19] See the press release at www.usdoj.gov/opa/pr/2003/November/03_ag_624.htm.

[20] The high-strength organic fiber Zylon® (PBO fiber—poly-p-phenylene benzobisoxazole) is produced by and is a registered trademark of Toyobo Company, Ltd.

[21] See "For more information" at the end of this section.

[22] *NIJ 2005 Interim Requirements for Bullet-Resistant Body Armor* and a list of models that comply with the requirements are available at www.justnet.org/BatPro.

NIJ supports innovative approaches to crime prevention and reduction. Some of these programs have achieved breakthroughs in reducing juvenile gun violence by identifying crime "hot spots" and by building effective partnerships among Federal, State, and local levels of government, researchers, and the community.

NIJ also may issue Body Armor Standard Advisory Notices to identify body armor materials that, based on NIJ review, appear to create a risk of death or serious injury as a result of degraded ballistic performance.[23] Any body armor model that contains any material listed in such an advisory will be deemed no longer NIJ-compliant unless and until the manufacturer satisfies NIJ that the model will maintain its ballistic performance over its declared warranty period.

NIJ will continue its body armor research and evaluation program to:

- Determine what additional modifications to the requirements of NIJ's compliance testing program may be appropriate.
- Better understand the degradation mechanisms affecting the performance of new and existing ballistic materials.
- Develop methods for testing the ongoing performance of body armor.

For more information

- "NIJ's Bullet-Resistant Vest Standard Reaches Milestone," *NIJ Journal* 249 (July 2003), available at www.ncjrs.gov/pdffiles1/jr000249e.pdf.
- The Bulletproof Vest Partnership was created by Congress in 1998.[24] Details are at www.ojp.usdoj.gov/bvpbasi/docs/08_18_05BAI_AdvisoryNotice.doc.
- *Status Report to the Attorney General on Body Armor Safety Initiative Testing and Activities*, Special Report, March 2004, NCJ 204534, available at www.ojp.usdoj.gov/bvpbasi/docs/ArmorReport.pdf.
- *Supplement I: Status Report to the Attorney General on Body Armor Safety Initiative Testing and Activities*, Special Report, December 2004, NCJ 207605, available at www.ncjrs.gov/pdffiles1/nij/207605.pdf.
- *Third Status Report to the Attorney General on Body Armor Safety Initiative Testing and Activities*, Special Report, August 2005, NCJ 210418, available at www.ojp.usdoj.gov/bvpbasi/docs/SupplementII_08_12_05.pdf.

[23] Body Armor Standard Advisory Notice #01-2005 was issued in August 2005; see www.ojp.usdoj.gov/bvpbasi/docs/08_18_05BAI_AdvisoryNotice.doc.

[24] 42 USC §§379611–379611-3.

Crime prevention and reduction

NIJ supports innovative approaches to crime prevention and reduction. Some of these programs have achieved breakthroughs in reducing juvenile gun violence by identifying crime "hot spots" and by building effective partnerships among Federal, State, and local levels of government, researchers, and the community. Innovation continued in 2005, spurred by new threats and improved collaboration among Federal, State, and local agencies.

Safeguarding communities. NIJ sponsors research to determine what types of interventions best reduce crime in the Nation's communities. Successful initiatives in several major cities led the way with innovative problem-solving approaches and partnerships formed to target *local* crime problems.[25] In 2001, Project Safe Neighborhoods (PSN) built upon this work by establishing local problem-solving initiatives to reduce gun violence, spearheaded by United States Attorneys.[26]

For the last 2 years, NIJ has been conducting peer-to-peer training on strategic problem solving for all 94 PSN task forces. NIJ is also providing technical assistance to individual districts in the implementation, operation, and assessment of PSN initiatives.[27] Researchers are conducting case studies to determine to what extent the PSN multiagency, strategic problem-solving model is working. Evaluators are looking at the program's impact on gun crime and the criminal justice system.

Improving police-researcher partnerships. For several decades, NIJ has encouraged cooperation between researchers and police departments to study policing practices and develop and evaluate intervention strategies to address local crime problems. Despite notable successes,[28] a roundtable sponsored by the International Association of Chiefs of Police found that:

> The powerful potentials of law enforcement/researcher partnerships haven't yet been fully realized ...[O]nly a small minority of the 17,580 law enforcement agencies across the country have even realized the benefits of research partnerships.[29]

[25] See *NIJ FY 2004 Annual Report,* NCJ 209274: 27–29, available at www.ncjrs.gov/pdffiles1/nij/209274.pdf. Also see Russell-Einhorn, M., *Fighting Urban Crime: The Evolution of Federal-Local Collaboration,* December 2003, NCJ 197040, available at www.ncjrs.gov/pdffiles1/nij/197040.pdf.

[26] More background is provided in *NIJ FY 2004 Annual Report* 28–29; also see www.psn.gov.

[27] For more information, see www.cj.msu.edu/~outreach/psn/psntechassist.html.

[28] Examples include the Boston Ceasefire program, NIJ's Strategic Approaches to Community Safety Initiative (SACSI), and PSN. See *NIJ FY 2004 Annual Report:* 27–28, and Roehl et al. cited at the end of this section.

[29] See *Unresolved Problems and Powerful Potentials, Improving Partnerships Between Law Enforcement Leaders and University Based Researchers, Recommendations from the IACP 2003 Roundtable,* August 2004, available at www.iacp.org/research/LawEnforcement-UniversityPartnership.pdf.

NIJ is working with its practitioner and governmental partners to meet this need. Police-researcher partnerships require that both parties reexamine established practices and adapt to changing circumstances while collaborating with Federal, State, and local authorities and community-based groups to implement and evaluate programs.[30] NIJ is currently funding the International Association of Chiefs of Police to develop guidelines for researchers and police practitioners on effective implementation of such partnerships.

Identity theft. "Identity theft" and "identity fraud" refer to crimes in which someone wrongfully obtains and uses another person's personal data through fraud or deceptive means, typically for economic gain.[31] Victims may suffer financial losses and damaged credit and may even be falsely accused of a crime committed in their name.

Identity thieves use many means to obtain valid personal information, from stealing mail to "phishing."[32] Identity theft presents significant challenges for law enforcement because crimes committed may cross jurisdictions and may be confounded with other crimes—such as credit card fraud, Internet scams, and even terrorism. NIJ is supporting the development of technologies to help law enforcement investigate computer-related crimes (see "Project Who?").

Although identity theft affected an estimated 3.6 million households in 2004 alone,[33] little social science research has been conducted on this crime. To develop a research agenda for identity theft, NIJ held a focus group meeting[34] and commissioned a comprehensive report[35] that reviewed the available research and data. The report identifies types of identity theft, the myriad issues and problems associated with this broad category of crime, and areas for future research, including the need for more information about offenders. NIJ recently funded ethnographic research on identity theft offenders that explores the measures they employ, their associations with other criminal activity, the apparent rewards and risks they associate with identity theft, and their awareness of and responses to law enforcement. NIJ is also helping the Office for Victims of Crime produce an Identity Theft Resource Guide for victims' service organizations.[36]

[30] See Kellermann, A.L., D. Fuqua-Whitley, and C.S. Parramore, *Reducing Gun Violence: Community Problem Solving in Atlanta*, NCJ 209800 (release scheduled for July 2006).

[31] For an overview of identity theft crime issues and resources, see www.ncjrs.gov/spotlight/identity_theft/summary.html.

[32] "Phishing" refers to an e-mail scam that attempts to obtain valid Social Security numbers or account information by convincing the victim the sender is a legitimate financial organization.

[33] The National Crime and Victimization Survey, sponsored by the Bureau of Justice Statistics, only began tracking prevalence of identity theft crime in 2004. See www.ojp.usdoj.gov/bjs/abstract/it04.htm.

[34] Held in Washington, DC, in January 2005, the meeting included researchers, practitioners from Federal and local law enforcement, prosecutors, victim service providers, banking and credit card company representatives, motor vehicle administrators, victims, and representatives from other Federal agencies involved in combating identity theft.

[35] Newman, Graeme R., and M.M. McNally, *Identity Theft Literature Review*, July 2005, NCJ 210459, available at www.ncjrs.gov/pdffiles1/nij/grants/210459.pdf.

[36] The publication will be completed in 2006.

Project Who?

Awarded in 2005, NIJ's "Project Who?" will develop a model framework for the management, analysis, and visualization of identity theft crime data stored in stand-alone law enforcement databases and on the Internet. The goal is a user-friendly online tool to improve the capability of law enforcement to address this increasingly common but difficult-to-track crime. A prototype will be fielded in late summer 2006 with several San Diego police departments.

Crime mapping. The combination of geographical information systems with spatial data analysis tools helps crime analysts measure and analyze "hot spots" (areas where data indicate crimes most frequently occur) to improve tactical and strategic decisionmaking in local law enforcement agencies. In August 2005, NIJ published *Mapping Crime: Understanding Hot Spots*, a technical guide to mapping and analyzing areas that experience increased criminal activity.

NIJ's Mapping and Analysis for Public Safety program held its eighth annual Crime Mapping Research Conference on September 7–10, 2005.[37] Researchers and practitioners took crime mapping beyond the question of "where" to an examination of "why" spatial patterns of crime and hot spots occur. Other topics included geographic profiling—a technique that helps law enforcement locate a serial offender's base of operation (e.g., home, work)—and improvements in software tools for law enforcement practitioners.

For more information

- The fourth report in NIJ's Reducing Gun Violence series was released in 2005: *Reducing Gun Violence: Operation Ceasefire in Los Angeles*, Tita, G.E., K.J. Riley, G. Ridgeway, and P.W. Greenwood, Research Report, February 2005, NCJ 192378, available at www.ncjrs.gov/pdffiles1/nij/192378.pdf.

- *Strategic Approaches to Community Safety Initiative (SACSI) in 10 U.S. Cities: The Building Blocks for Project Safe Neighborhoods*, Roehl, J., D.P. Rosenbaum, S.K. Costello, J.R. Coldren, A.M. Schuck, L. Cunard, and D.R. Forde, February 2006, NCJ 212866, available at www.ncjrs.gov/pdffiles1/nij/grants/212866.pdf.

- *Identity Theft Literature Review*, Newman, Graeme R., and M.M. McNally, July 2005, NCJ 210459, available at www.ncjrs.gov/pdffiles1/nij/grants/210459.pdf.

- *Mapping Crime: Understanding Hot Spots*, Eck, J.E., S. Chainey, J.G. Cameron, M. Leitner, and R.E. Wilson, Special Report, August 2005, NCJ 209393, available at www.NCJRS.gov/pdffiles1/nij/209393.pdf.

[37] The conference was held in Savannah, Georgia, with support from the National Law Enforcement and Corrections Technology Center. Conference topics are listed at www.ojp.gov/nij/maps.

Law enforcement professionals need to know what works, what doesn't, and how to use new tools and technologies effectively. NIJ's Office of Science and Technology develops and evaluates emerging technologies and creates standards and requirements for their use.

NIJ's Technical Working Groups (TWGs)

Composed of practitioner experts, TWGs meet at least twice a year to discuss the needs of the field and help NIJ set priorities. Current TWG topics are:

- *Biometrics.*
- *Body Armor.*
- *Communications Technologies.*
- *Community Corrections.*
- *Cyber-Crime.*
- *DNA Forensics.*
- *Explosives.*
- *General Forensics.*
- *Geospatial Technologies.*
- *Information-Led Policing.*
- *Institutional Corrections.*
- *Less-Lethal Technologies.*
- *Modeling and Simulation.*
- *Personnel Protection.*
- *Pursuit Management.*
- *School Safety.*
- *Sensors and Surveillance.*

Law enforcement tools and technology

New tools and technologies promise to improve security and help law enforcement identify, locate, and apprehend criminals. Some of these technologies are still experimental; others are in use, although relatively untested. Law enforcement professionals need to know what works, what doesn't, and how to use new tools and technologies effectively. NIJ's Office of Science and Technology develops and evaluates emerging technologies and creates standards and requirements for their use, in tandem with other government agencies, the military, academia, and industry.

NIJ's R&D process. To better identify practitioners' key technology needs and transfer mature technology to the field, NIJ implemented a management plan in 2005 that aligned its National Law Enforcement and Corrections Technology Center system with the agency's research, development, test, and evaluation (RDT&E) process. Practitioner-based technical working groups (TWGs) were established within the centers for each of the agency's technology portfolios. With oversight from the Law Enforcement and Corrections Technology Advisory Council, TWGs now define the functional requirements for each portfolio and, thus, the basis for NIJ's strategic planning.

The NIJ RDT&E process has five phases: (1) identify needs and operational requirements; (2) plan a multiyear research program in each area of need; (3) perform research and development from concept to field-ready prototype; (4) demonstrate, test, and evaluate technology; and (5) assist practitioners in the use of the new technology.

NIJ's annual budget implementation cycle now integrates the TWGs, which meet at least twice a year. This cycle was fully implemented for the first time in 2005. Technology requirements for FY 2006 science and technology solicitations were derived from the TWGs' recommendations.

FY 2005 solicitations encouraged technological innovation to enhance law enforcement operations and safety, national security, antiterrorism strategies and tactics, and critical incident response. Technologies currently under investigation include less-lethal weapons; biometrics (fast capture of fingerprints and palm prints, face recognition, iris readers); sensors (advanced weapons detectors, license plate readers, gunshot detection systems, through-the-wall surveillance); interoperability solutions (cognitive radios, satellite communications); and tools to defeat improvised explosive devices.[38]

Police use of force and less-lethal technologies. Law enforcement officers are authorized to use force in specific, limited circumstances. Officers typically face numerous circumstances during their careers when the use of force is appropriate—for example, when making arrests, restraining unruly combatants, or controlling disruptive demonstrations. NIJ identifies and evaluates new and improved devices that can minimize the risk of death and injury to law enforcement officers, suspects, prisoners, and the general public. Tools such as electro-muscular disruption devices[39] give police and corrections personnel an alternative to the use of lethal force. Today, more than 5,000 police departments use less-lethal technologies. However, the increase in deployment has raised safety and other concerns, which NIJ research is investigating.

For example, in 2005, NIJ worked with the International Association of Chiefs of Police to develop a model policy and best practices guide for electro-muscular disruption devices.[40] NIJ also solicited proposals for research and evaluation of the impact of less-lethal technologies on use-of-force incidents. Two studies are currently examining how risks to officers, bystanders, and suspects change or vary as a result of the type of strategy, tactic, policy, or technology that an officer employs to manage a threatening situation. Researchers also are developing safer, more effective less-lethal technologies, including some that employ radio waves and coherent light.

[38] FY 2005 grant awards are listed in appendix B. FY 2005 solicitations are available at www.ojp.usdoj.gov/nij/funding/expired/fund2005exp.htm.

[39] TASERs® are examples of electro-muscular disruption devices.

[40] *Electro-Muscular Disruption Technology: A Nine-Step Strategy for Effective Deployment,* April 2005, available in print or at www.theiacp.org/research/RCDCuttingEdgeTech.htm.

In April, NIJ and the Bureau of Justice Assistance hosted a symposium to present State and local law enforcement practitioners and policymakers with the most up-to-date research on less-lethal technologies and to seek counsel from the field. NIJ continues to participate in meetings on this topic hosted by the Commission on Accreditation for Law Enforcement Agencies.

Pursuit management. NIJ-sponsored researchers are investigating vehicle-stopping or pursuit management technologies—an important goal for law enforcement agencies seeking ways to stop rather than pursue fleeing vehicles. Development and evaluation is under way of two promising technologies that immobilize a moving car by discharging an electromagnetic field or radio waves to disable a vehicle's electronic components.[41]

Biometrics. The NIJ Biometrics program is active in laboratory research, development, and evaluation; system enhancements; and standards development. Law enforcement's priorities for biometric technologies include:

- Rapidly and accurately recording fingerprints and palm prints for enhanced criminal identification and civil background checks.

- Confirming and fixing the identity of criminals within the justice system.

- Identifying known offenders from video and audio surveillance.

- Controlling physical access to facilities and logical access to computers and data systems.

NIJ grantees are examining technologies for fast capture of fingerprints or palm prints (see chapter 2). Image quality must meet or exceed specifications set by the National Institute of Standards and Technology and the Federal Bureau of Investigation. Prototypes are expected within 2 years. Other biometrics projects are examining face, eye, speech, hand geometry, and even ear recognition, as well as the identification of persons through video or audio surveillance. NIJ plays a leadership role in DOJ's Biometrics Cooperative and participates in the White House National Science and Technology Council Subcommittee on Biometrics.

[41] See *Pursuit Management Task Force*, August 1998, NCJ 184352, available at www.ncjrs.gov/pdffiles/fs000225.pdf, for a brief description of the pursuit management technologies under study and why they were chosen.

Sensors. Law enforcement and corrections agencies use sensors for detecting contraband (especially weapons), locating individuals, securing facilities (from schools to seaports), and running tactical operations such as hostage rescue. NIJ sponsors sensor research and development in close collaboration with other agencies within the U.S. Department of Defense, the U.S. Department of Homeland Security, and the U.S. Department of Energy. These projects include development of sensors that can from a safe distance detect handguns and suicide bomb belts concealed on an individual and development of the capability to remotely locate and track individuals inside buildings. In 2005, with the Los Angeles Police Department Bomb Squad, NIJ demonstrated a prototype device to romotoly dotoct ouicide bombers.

Other sensor projects include a collaborative effort with the U.S. Coast Guard and 20 other agencies to evaluate x-ray surveillance technology to protect U.S. ports[42] and development of a portable camera able to instantly read the license plates of moving cars and automatically query stolen car databases.

Tools to deal with improvised explosive devices (IEDs). NIJ is working to provide improved tools to help State and local bomb squads deal with IEDs. Conducted in close collaboration with the Federal Bureau of Investigation, the Bureau of Alcohol, Tobacco, Firearms, and Explosives, and other agencies, this program is studying some of the more intractable types of IEDs, such as vehicle- and radio-controlled bombs. In 2005, together with the Science and Technology Directorate of the U.S. Department of Homeland Security and the U.S. Department of Defense's Combating Terrorism Technology Support Office's Technical Support Working Group, NIJ delivered an improved means of defeating radio-controlled bombs. This device will be evaluated by State and local bomb squads in 2006.

A prototype bomb squad information-sharing system was also deployed in Boston, Philadelphia, and New York City. This demonstration will be expanded to the West Coast in 2006.

[42] Bulk explosives detection technologies are discussed in Thiesan, L, D. Dannum, D.W. Murray, and J.E. Parmeter, *Survey of Commercially Available Explosives Detection Technologies and Equipment 2004*, February 2005, NCJ 208861, available at www.ncjrs.gov/pdffiles1/nij/grants/208861.pdf.

Interoperability. Police officers, firefighters, emergency medical personnel, and other public safety officials often cannot depend on wireless radio communications in an emergency. Lack of communication can severely hinder a coordinated response to natural disasters, catastrophic accidents, and criminal actions. NIJ's Communications Technology (CommTech) program is helping to bridge gaps in emergency communications by identifying and developing interoperability solutions that use open architecture standards for voice, data, image, and video communication systems. The goal is to allow multiple parties to exchange information "on the spot." CommTech research and development efforts are concentrated on Software Defined Radio, cognitive radio, Voice-over-Internet-Protocol, Advanced Wireless Voice and Data, and in-building location and communication technologies.[43]

Developing standards is vital to addressing the issue of public safety interoperability. NIJ is directly involved in the development of national standards for digital two-way radio technology and funds approximately 20 interoperability research, development, and demonstration projects a year, devoting about $13 million to the CommTech portfolio. The agency works closely with the U.S. Department of Homeland Security's SAFECOM program[44] and many other Federal, State, and local partners. Through its CommTech program, NIJ provided interoperability assistance for the 2001 and 2005 Presidential Inaugurations, the Hurricane Rita response, and the Moussaoui trial. CommTech staff developed an interoperability plan for the 2006 opening of the Woodrow Wilson Bridge in the Washington, DC, metropolitan area.

For more information

- NIJ's Technology and Research Development Web site: www.ojp.usdoj.gov/nij/sciencetech/welcome.html. NLECTC Web site: www.nlectc.org.

- *Electro-Muscular Disruption Technology: A Nine-Step Strategy for Effective Deployment,* April 2005, available at www.iacp.org/research/rcdcuttingedgetech.htm.

[43] These efforts are being undertaken in close cooperation with the U.S. Department of Homeland Security's SAFECOM Program Office.

[44] See the SAFECOM Web site at www.safecomprogram.gov/SAFECOM.

- NIJ's less-lethal technology grant projects are described at www.ojp.usdoj. gov/nij/topics/lesslethal/projects.htm.

- Biometrics Catalog Web site: www.biometricscatalog.org/default.aspx.

- "A Safe Port in the Storm," *TechBeat* (Spring 2005), available at www.nlectc. org/techbeat/spring2005/SafePort.pdf.

- CommTech research is discussed at www.ojp.usdoj.gov/nij/topics/commtech/ funding.htm; a list of publications is available at www.ojp.usdoj.gov/nij/ topics/commtech/pubs.htm.

- Fact sheets on radio spectrum and Voice-over-Internet-Protocol were released in early 2006, and more are being developed. See www.ojp.usdoj. gov/nij/topics/commtech/welcome.html.

Corrections

With nearly 7 million people in jail or prison or on probation or parole at the close of 2004,[45] corrections officials face many challenges. NIJ has sponsored research, development, and evaluation initiatives to address mental health issues in institutional corrections, correctional officer safety,[46] community corrections issues such as parole officer stress and prisoner reentry, and most recently, sexual assault in prisons.

Prevalence and impact of prison sexual violence. In response to the Prison Rape Elimination Act,[47] NIJ is building a research agenda to fill the large gaps in knowledge about sexual violence and victimization in correctional settings. In 2005, NIJ funded a study in Ohio that will examine the effect that prison rape has on a victim's ability to readjust to society upon release. The Ohio Department of Corrections and Rehabilitation requires inmates who do not come to the full term of their sentence to live in halfway houses for a period of time prior to release. This study will provide insight into inmates' experiences during their stay in these halfway houses, including documenting possible cases of victimization of persons housed there.

[45] *Corrections Statistics*, Bureau of Justice Statistics, available at www.ojp.usdoj.gov/bjs/correct.htm.

[46] See *NIJ FY 2004 Annual Report*, NCJ 209274: 22, available at www.ncjrs.gov/pdffiles1/nij/209274.pdf.

[47] The Prison Rape Elimination Act of 2003. See *NIJ FY 2004 Annual Report* 23.

Inmate rehabilitation programs are recognizing that women have different needs than men, specifically greater social, emotional, and physical challenges that affect their rehabilitation and reentry into society.

Women in Corrections

In 2004, the number of women in prisons and jails was 183,400 (out of 2,131,180 total inmates in the Nation).[50] The adult female jail population has grown an average of 7 percent annually over the past 10 years, while the adult male inmate population has grown 4.2 percent annually. An increasing percentage of female inmates were convicted of violent offenses: 17 percent in 2002 (compared to 26.5 percent of male inmates). In 2004, about 1 of every 8 adults on parole and almost 1 of every 4 probationers were women. More than 50 percent of women in jail report being physically or sexually abused before incarceration, compared to approximately 10 percent of men. Women are less likely than men to have been prior offenders, but are more likely to have had a drug-related offense.[51]

[48] Glaze, L.E., and S. Palla, *Probation and Parole in the United States, 2004*, Bureau of Justice Statistics, November 2005, NCJ 210676, available at www.ojp.usdoj.gov/bjs/pub/pdf/ppus04.pdf.

[49] The SVORI study will be completed in 2008; learn more at www.svori-evaluation.org.

[50] See *Prison Statistics*, Bureau of Justice Statistics, available at www.ojp.usdoj.gov/bjs/prisons.htm. Also see Harrison, P.M., and A.J. Beck, *Prison and Jail Inmates at Midyear 2004*, Bureau of Justice Statistics, April 2005, NCJ 208801, available at www.ojp.usdoj.gov/bjs/pub/pdf/pjim04.pdf.

[51] From the Bureau of Justice Statistics: James, D.J., *Profile of Jail Inmates, 2002*, revised October 12, 2004, available at www.ojp.usdoj.gov/bjs/pub/pdf/pji02.pdf; Glaze, L.E., and S. Palla (see note 48); and Wilson, D.J., and T. Hughes, *Reentry Trends in the United States 2002*, revised April 2004, available at www.ojp.usdoj.gov/bjs/reentry/reentry.htm.

Because sexual victimization in corrections often occurs in conjunction with other violent acts, NIJ released a solicitation in 2005 to foster research examining sexual violence within the context of other violent behavior perpetrated by prison inmates.

Prisoner reentry. NIJ seeks to improve corrections by helping offenders return to the community. The number of adult men and women in the United States who were being supervised on probation or parole reached a new high of 4,916,480 by the end of 2004. An estimated 650,000 prisoners were released from prisons and jails last year.[48] Thus, prisoner reentry issues are not abstract or remote for most communities.

NIJ has several projects under way related to corrections, probation and parole, prisoners and former prisoners, and children of prisoners.

Serious and violent offender reentry. Two-thirds of released prisoners reoffend, often committing violent crimes. To meet this challenge, DOJ, in partnership with the U.S. Departments of Labor, Housing and Urban Development, and Health and Human Services, established the Serious and Violent Offender Reentry Initiative (SVORI) in 2002. NIJ is conducting a 5-year evaluation of SVORI, one of the largest program evaluations in its history.[49]

SVORI has awarded more than $100 million to 69 grantees who are running 89 programs intended to reduce recidivism by improving the employment opportunities, housing options, and health outcomes of participating released prisoners. Researchers are evaluating the programs' relative costs and benefits, as well as whether participants demonstrate better outcomes such as reduced recidivism.

Reentry programs for women inmates. The number of women entering the correctional system has steadily climbed over the past decade (see "Women in Corrections"). Inmate rehabilitation programs are recognizing that women have different needs than men, specifically greater social, emotional, and physical challenges that affect their rehabilitation and reentry into society. NIJ evaluations demonstrate that these programs show promise in helping women overcome drug addiction and posttraumatic stress disorder through education and job training, life skills training, and emotional and mental health counseling.

Why do some women continue to recidivate after participating in a rehabilitation program? Researchers have identified problems with an abusive partner encountered after release, lack of education or income, and inability to deal with the stress of daily life as possible factors. One study found that a female inmate was at higher risk to recidivate if she had a history of emotional/psychological difficulties, had contemplated suicide, or had difficulty controlling her temper. Recognizing that women have different treatment needs than men and focusing on women-specific issues and aftercare can help women successfully reintegrate into society.[52]

For more information

- "Attorney General Announces $6.7 Million to Help Ex-Offenders Reentering Communities," U.S. Department of Justice Press Release, September 20, 2004, available at www.usdoj.gov/opa/pr/2004/September/04_ojp_630.htm.

- *Women Offenders*, Greenfield, L.A., and T.L. Snell, Bureau of Justice Statistics, Special Report, December 1999 (updated October 2000), NCJ 175688, available at www.ojp.usdoj.gov/bjs/pub/pdf/wo.pdf.

- "Drug Treatment and Reentry for Incarcerated Women," Wells, D., and L. Bright, *Corrections Today* 67(7) (December 2005): 98–99, 111; available at www.ncjrs.gov/pdffiles1/nij/212776.pdf.

- "Reentry Programs for Women Inmates," *NIJ Journal* 252 (July 2005), available at www.ojp.usdoj.gov/nij/journals/252/reentry.html.

[52] "Reentry Programs for Women Inmates," *NIJ Journal* 252 (July 2005): 2–7, available at www.ojp.usdoj.gov/nij/journals/252/reentry.html, discusses the programs and findings from these complex studies.

Courtroom →

Progress in Understanding and Fighting Victimization

NIJ's Office of Research and Evaluation sponsors the Violence Against Women and Family Violence Research and Evaluation Program.[53] The program's objectives are to promote the safety of women and other family members and to increase the effectiveness of the criminal justice system's response to family violence. Researchers are identifying the risk and protective factors associated with violence against women and family violence, evaluating promising prevention and intervention programs, and disseminating findings to the field.[54]

Promising studies

NIJ funds research on violence against women, domestic and intimate partner abuse, elder abuse, and sexual assault among certain populations (e.g., college students) and within culturally diverse communities (see "Understanding the Needs of Deaf Victims"). The agency maintains an online compendium describing grants in this field from 1993 to the present.[55]

Elder abuse. Knowledge about the extent of abuse of the elderly is limited, largely because no "gold standard test" exists for abuse or neglect.[56] Practitioners working with the elderly must rely on forensic markers—but caregivers and even doctors often are not trained to distinguish between injuries caused by mistreatment and those caused by accident, illness, or aging. Because many elderly individuals suffer from diseases or conditions that can mask or mimic indicators of mistreatment, the presence of these indicators may not send up a red flag for physicians and medical examiners. Doctors caring for elders also often fail to recognize how psychological conditions—such as depression and dementia—place an elderly individual at greater risk of abuse.

An NIJ study released in 2005 examined the role of forensic markers in identifying elder abuse and recommended additional research to further refine these indicators.[57] In FY 2005, NIJ awarded several grants concerning elder abuse, including a continuation of research to examine bruising as a forensic marker

---

[53] Human trafficking victimization is discussed in chapter 5.

[54] See NIJ's Violence Against Women and Family Violence Web site at www.ojp.usdoj.gov/nij/vawprog/welcome.html.

[55] See www.ojp.usdoj.gov/nij/vawprog/vaw_portfolio.pdf.

[56] Dyer, C.B., M.T. Connolly, and P. McFeeley, "The Clinical and Medical Forensics of Elder Abuse and Neglect," *Elder Mistreatment: Abuse, Neglect, and Exploitation in an Aging America,* ed. R.J. Bonnie and R.B. Wallace, Washington, DC: National Academies Press, 2003: 343.

[57] See Lindbloom et al., cited at the end of this chapter.

Police contact or a protective order reduced the risk of intimate partner reassault by as much as 70 percent.

Understanding the Needs of Deaf Victims

A recent NIJ project recruited Deaf persons to participate in a study of their experiences as victims of sexual assault. Police response and service needs were also evaluated. Researchers found that interaction with the police could be frustrating for Deaf victims, who were more likely to disclose sexual abuse to service providers. Researchers also found gaps between the perceptions of the victims and the hearing service providers who assisted them in the aftermath of sexual victimization. A report will be released in 2006.

of abuse. Other investigations in NIJ's portfolio of ongoing research into elder mistreatment include a study on the markers associated with deaths of elderly residents in long-term care facilities, a study examining factors that place an elder at risk for abuse or neglect, and a study examining medical examiner practices in identifying cases of elder abuse.

Sexual assault between intimate partners. Although physical abuse within intimate partner relationships has been widely studied, less attention has been paid to sexual violence within these relationships. NIJ-funded researchers completed a study in FY 2005 that examined a sample of women who had obtained protective orders. Researchers found that 68 percent of these participants reported being sexually assaulted at least once by their intimate partner.[58] Police contact or a protective order reduced the risk of intimate partner reassault by as much as 70 percent. Not contacting police after the first assault doubled a victim's risk of reassault; not applying for a protective order tripled the risk of reassault.

Perhaps even more startling was the study's finding that 88 percent of the participants' children—64 percent of whom were under age 3—were exposed to the violence against their mothers. These children "showed the same degree of depressive behaviors as children under treatment for depression, and appreciably more behavioral problems than" youngsters of mothers who were physically but not sexually abused. Only 30 percent of these children received counseling. The researchers recommended training service providers to assess victims for type and frequency of intimate partner sexual assault, to help victims deal with the consequences of the assault, and inform victims about their increased risks for reassault and the potentially harmful effects on their children.

In FY 2005, an NIJ-funded study used data from the Project on Human Development in Chicago Neighborhoods (PHDCN)[59] to examine the effects of childhood exposure to intimate partner violence. Severe violence perpetrated by the male partner was found to have a particularly strong effect on the child's externalizing behavior (delinquency, aggression, or substance use). The largest effect on internalizing behavior (depression, anxiety, and feelings of worthless-

[58] See McFarlane, J., and A. Malecha, *Sexual Assault Among Intimates: Frequency, Consequences, and Treatments,* October 2005, NCJ 211678, available at www.ncjrs.gov/pdffiles1/nij/grants/211678.pdf.

[59] See *Intricate Pathways: The Project on Human Development in Chicago Neighborhoods,* Harvard University, 2004, available at www.hms.harvard.edu/chase/projects/chicago/about/intricate.html. When PHDCN began in 1995, children were ages 0–18. Data used for this study were collected from 1995 to 1997.

ness) was severe intimate partner violence perpetrated by the woman. Intimate partner violence was also found to increase anxiety in children, leading to behavior problems. Clinical interventions with children exposed to domestic violence should focus on reducing anxiety and treating stress-related disorders. This study also showed that children exposed to domestic violence who have strong bonds with their primary caregiver are less likely to demonstrate externalizing behavior.

Evaluating SANE programs. Sexual Assault Nurse Examiner (SANE) programs are proliferating, with the endorsement of criminal justice practitioners and policymakers. However, little is known about whether SANE programs increase prosecution of sexual assault cases. A current NIJ grant is exploring this question. Researchers are examining the interrelationships among prosecutors, police, victim advocates, and victims/survivors and will develop a program evaluation toolkit for practitioners to assess post-SANE systems change in their communities.[60]

Batterer intervention programs. The concept of intervening with batterers in order to change their behavior emerged as a result of frustration among shelter workers who witnessed women being revictimized after returning home to their same male partners or watched batterers move on to new victims. Shelter advocates began to develop group programs for male batterers in the late 1970's.[61]

Researchers agree that offenders who complete programs for batterers have lower rearrest rates than those who do not. However, the official rates for reabuse are significantly lower than victim's reports of reabuse. Batterer intervention program evaluations have yielded inconsistent results. Some batterers drop out of the program, and some continue to abuse repeatedly.

Over the past decade, NIJ has funded 15 projects on batterer intervention. An NIJ study completed in FY 2005 found that batterer intervention groups devoting more thematic focus to cultural issues specific to African American men are likely to be as effective as, or no more effective than, traditional groups consisting of either all African American men or racially/ethnically mixed clientele. This

[60] For more information about SANE programs, see Littel, K., *Sexual Assault Nurse Examiner (SANE) Programs: Improving the Community Response to Sexual Assault Victims,* April 2001, NCJ 186366, available at www.ovc.gov/publications/bulletins/sane_4_2001/186366.pdf.

[61] See Jackson, S., "Batterer Intervention Programs," *Batterer Intervention Programs: Where Do We Go From Here?* June 2003, NCJ 195079: 1–4, available at www.ncjrs.gov/pdffiles1/nij/195079.pdf.

finding of essentially "no difference" is not a final answer, however, since culturally focused counseling also needs to be tested with other racial and ethnic groups.

A second study found that a specialized domestic violence caseload handled by probation officers trained in domestic violence led to lower rates of reoffending and longer arrest-free periods for most offenders in the program.

Many questions about the efficacy of batterer intervention programs remain, with important implications for the safety of battered women and their children.[62] NIJ's research agenda includes developing assessment instruments, testing a system that addresses specific batterer needs, evaluating programs that use electronic monitoring and Global Positioning Systems, and testing the impact of swift and certain response to violations of protective orders and/or probation conditions.

For more information

- *Results From an Elder Abuse Prevention Experiment in New York City*, Davis, R.C., and J. Medina-Ariza, Research in Brief, September 2001, NCJ 188675, available at www.ncjrs.gov/pdffiles1/nij/188675.pdf.

- Office for Victims of Crime Web page on elder abuse: www.ojp.usdoj.gov/ovc/publications/infores/elder/welcome.html.

- *The Role of Forensic Science in Identification of Mistreatment Deaths in Long-Term Care Facilities*, Lindbloom, E., J. Brandt, C. Hawes, C. Phillips, D. Zimmerman, J. Robinson, B. Bowers, and P. McFeeley, April 2005, NCJ 209334, available at www.ncjrs.gov/pdffiles1/nij/grants/209334.pdf.

- "Does Batterers' Treatment Work? A Meta-Analytic Review of Domestic Violence Treatment," Babcock, J.C., C.E. Green, and C. Robie, *Clinical Psychology Review* 23(8) (2004): 1023–1053.

[62] For estimated prevalence of battering, see Rennison, C.M., and S. Welchans, *Intimate Partner Violence*, Bureau of Justice Statistics, May 2000 (revised January 31, 2002), available at www.ojp.usdoj.gov/bjs/pub/pdf/ipv.pdf.

- *Violence Against Women: Synthesis of Research on Offender Interventions*, Saunders, D.G., and R.M. Hamill, September 2003, NCJ 201222, available at www.ncjrs.gov/pdffiles1/nij/grants/201222.pdf.

- *Full Report of the Prevalence, Incidence, and Consequences of Violence Against Women: Findings From the National Violence Against Women Survey*, Tjaden, P., and N. Thoennes, November 2000, NCJ 183781, available at www.ncjrs.gov/pdffiles1/nij/183781.pdf.

- "Assessing Risk Factors for Intimate Partner Homicide," Campbell, J.C., C.R. Block, C. Sachs, D. Webster, D. Campbell, F. Gary, J. Koziol-McLain, J. McFarlane, M.A. Curry, and P. Sharps, and "Intimate Partner Homicide. An Overview," Zahn, M.A., *NIJ Journal* 250 (November 2003), available at www.ncjrs.gov/pdffiles1/jr000250.pdf.

- "The Decline of Intimate Partner Homicide," Wells, W., and W. DeLeon Granadus, *NIJ Journal* 252 (July 2005), available at www.ojp.usdoj.gov/nij/journals/252/homicide.html.

- *Violence Against Women: Identifying Risk Factors*, Research in Brief, November 2004, NCJ 197019, available at www.ncjrs.gov/pdffiles1/nij/197019.pdf.

- *Do Batterer Intervention Programs Work? Two Studies*, Research for Practice, September 2003, NCJ 200331, available at www.ncjrs.gov/pdffiles1/nij/200331.pdf.

International Crime, at Home and Abroad

A striking phenomenon of our times is the merging of local and transnational crime. NIJ founded the International Center in 1998 to study transnational crime, evaluate its impact, and foster the exchange of knowledge and ideas with other nations. During the past 8 years, more than 800 foreign professionals from 95 countries have visited NIJ to learn more about its research programs.

NIJ is a member of the United Nations Network of Program Institutes. International Center staff visit UN offices in Vienna, Austria, annually to collaborate with other research centers around the world and to represent U.S. crime and justice interests.[63]

The Center employs several techniques to identify the most pressing research questions. These include:

- Meetings of expert researchers and practitioners on topics of interest.

- Feasibility studies involving short contracts, intramural research, exhaustive literature reviews, and interviews with key players to isolate unknowns.

- Surveys of crime reports from outside the United States to assess patterns, especially those that have not yet emerged in this country.

- Reviews of nongovernmental and intergovernmental reports on special topics that have not yet garnered significant attention in the United States.

- Analysis of disconnected cases involving the same crime in search of patterns and connections. For example, is recent gang or fraud activity sporadic, organized, or of a particular type or group?

International program activities cover terrorism, human trafficking, organized crime and corruption, emerging issues, international justice system issues, and transnational research and dissemination.

[63] In collaboration with the U.S. Department of State. For details, see www.ojp.usdoj.gov/nij/international/programs/un_activities.html.

Most cases involving terrorism or human trafficking in the United States have been discovered by local officials.

Terrorism

After September 11, 2001, NIJ sponsored research into what is known about terrorism, terrorists, and police responses to the terrorism threat. Researchers are building a comprehensive knowledge base concerning terrorism and transnational crimes. In 2006, the International Center will sponsor a conference where NIJ grantees will present their findings to State and local criminal justice and homeland security professionals.

The Center's mission corresponds closely with DOJ's mission to prevent terrorism and with NIJ's efforts to assist State and local criminal justice practitioners and policymakers. This merging of purpose results from the fact that international crimes are often detected and best understood at the local level. Most cases involving terrorism or human trafficking in the United States have been discovered by local officials.

Serious gaps exist in social science data related to terrorism. To address this problem, NIJ is focusing on a wide range of topics related to terrorism and the criminal justice system and is seeking input from the field. For example, one outgrowth of an NIJ workshop on suicide bombers in May 2004 was an award to the National Archive of Criminal Justice Data to compile every known terrorist incident into a database.[64]

NIJ has sponsored more than 18 terrorism research projects. Some key studies and findings are:

- A comprehensive RAND report on organizational learning within terrorist groups, including five case studies.

- A survey of local prosecutors conducted by the American Prosecutors Research Institute, which found that only a few prosecutors have defined their roles in responding to terrorism.

- An indepth analysis comparing the criminality of international jihad groups with domestic right-wing groups. The study identified distinguishing features

[64] NIJ is cosponsoring two terrorist-related databases, one tracking terrorism incidents worldwide and one tracking terrorism-related indictments in the United States.

of terrorist-oriented criminality and discovered that conventional criminal investigations are the most successful in detecting and prosecuting terrorism cases.[65]

- A study of relations between law enforcement and Arab American communities since 9/11, which identified both problems and promising practices to improve cooperation between the two groups.[66]

- An indepth study of informal value transfer systems[67] and money laundering as a means of financing terrorism.

- Case studies of law enforcement's response to 9/11 in New York City and Arlington County, Virginia, examining the two departments' responses to the 9/11 incidents and changes made since that time.

- A study of public-private police partnerships, examining how they operate and coordinate to protect against the threat of terrorism around ports.

- Case studies focusing on security and vulnerability issues in the rail and subway systems of London, Madrid, Moscow, Tokyo, and Washington, DC.

Human trafficking

Enslavement and forced labor have reemerged as a serious global problem in the 21st century. The U.S. Department of State estimates that 600,000 to 800,000 persons (mostly women and children) are forced or defrauded into slavery and transported across national borders each year. The United States has become a destination country, corresponding to an imbalance in the world labor market and the poor social standing of women and children in many countries.[68] Victims are most often exploited as prostitutes, sweat shop workers, farm laborers, or domestic servants. In response to the problem, Congress passed the Trafficking Victims Protection Act.[69]

NIJ is funding studies to develop better data to inform policymakers and criminal justice professionals on this issue. A meeting of experts in 2001 identified

[65] See Hamm, M.S., *Crimes Committed by Terrorist Groups: Theory, Research, and Prevention*, September 2005, NCJ 211203, available at www.ncjrs.gov/pdffiles1/nij/grants/211203.pdf.

[66] Henderson, N.J., C.W. Ortiz, N.F. Sugie, and J. Miller, *Engagement in a Time of Uncertainty: Relations Between Law Enforcement and Arab American Communities After September 11, 2001*, November 2005, available from the Vera Institute, at www.vera.org.

[67] Such as "hawala" systems that transfer funds from person to person without using banking or wire systems, often used by law-abiding immigrants and citizens to transfer money to relatives "back home." See Passas, N., "Law Enforcement Challenges in Hawala-Related Investigations," *Journal of Financial Crime* 12(2) (December 2004): 112–119.

[68] See the U.S. Department of State (DOS) fact sheet, May 24, 2004, at www.state.gov/r/pa/ei/rls/33109.htm. DOS publishes an annual report, *Trafficking in Persons*; 150 nations are listed as having some degree of trafficking activity. The 2005 report is at www.state.gov/g/tip/rls/tiprpt/2005. Quantifying this underground, often well-shielded criminal activity is still a subject of research. Estimates are largely educated guesses based on a combination of anecdotal information and hard data.

[69] 114 Stat. 1464, PL 106–386, October 28, 2000; the Act was strengthened in 2003. Access the statute at www.state.gov/documents/organization/10492.pdf.

Trafficking in the United States

An NIJ-sponsored project that examined stages in the process of human trafficking in the United States found that lack of awareness of victims' living and working conditions, lack of law enforcement training, and the public's demand for cheap goods and services all contribute to the problem.[72] Additional research is under way to identify patterns, determine the extent of the demand for forced labor in the United States, and evaluate ways to interdict and intervene.

some fundamental research needs in this area. Research topics subsequently funded include:

- Estimates of prevalence and trafficking flows in the United States.
- An evaluation of services available to victims.[70]
- Analysis of how the law enforcement and prosecution response can be improved, lessons learned from known cases, and characteristics of child survivors.[71]

Emerging issues

During the past few years, the areas of transnational crime that have emerged as growing problems include international gang activity; transnational fraud involving cyber-crime, intellectual property theft, and other white-collar crimes; and theft and smuggling of natural resources.

International gang activity. Long a focus of public concern in Los Angeles, the Mara Salvatrucha gang (MS-13) has gained national and international attention. Recent violent incidents attributed to MS-13 in the Washington, DC, metropolitan area received extensive media coverage and spawned new Federal and local law enforcement collaboration. For example, in 2005 the Federal Bureau of Investigation established an MS-13 task force and an intelligence-sharing initiative with Mexican authorities. NIJ has funded a study of the gang's structure and activities in three urban areas: Los Angeles, Washington, DC, and San Salvador.

Cyber-crime and intellectual property theft. Changes in how money and property are held, stored, and moved have created modern forms of fraud (e.g., identity theft, intellectual property theft, Internet scams). These crimes are easier to commit yet more difficult to detect, prevent, and punish. Several International Center studies on these issues were published in 2005.[73]

Theft and smuggling of natural resources. NIJ is funding two studies on this topic. The first concerns the illegal commercial trade in elephant ivory and rhinoceros horn that has resurfaced in eastern and southern Africa. Researchers are determining the extent and causes of the practice, developing a model of the covert supply chain, identifying the structure of smugglers' transnational

[70] Cosponsored with the Office for Victims of Crime.

[71] NIJ research projects on human trafficking are listed at www.ojp.usdoj.gov/nij/international/global_res.html.

[72] Bales, K., and S. Lize, *Trafficking in Persons in the United States*, November 2005, www.ncjrs.gov/pdffiles1/nij/grants/211980.pdf.

[73] The journal *Trends in Organized Crime* 8(4) (2005) features four articles on intellectual property theft based on research funded through NIJ's International Center.

networks and markets, and evaluating the effectiveness of U.S. legislation and law enforcement efforts.

The second study concerns the pathways of illegally harvested timber entering the United States. Researchers are examining where illegal lumbering occurs, how it is shipped across borders, and where it is "cleansed" before being sent to a legal market. A final report on this project is due in 2006.

For more information

- NIJ's International Center: www.ojp.usdoj.gov/nij/international/welcome.html.

- *Aptitude for Destruction, Volume 1: Organizational Learning in Terrorist Groups and Its Implications for Combating Terrorism,* Jackson, B.A., J.C. Baker, P. Chalk, R.K. Cragin, J.V. Parachini, and H.R. Trujillo, 2005, available at www.rand.org/pubs/monographs/MG331/index.html.

- *Aptitude for Destruction, Volume 2: Case Studies of Organizational Learning in Five Terrorist Groups,* Jackson, B.A., J.C. Baker, P. Chalk, R.K. Cragin, J.V. Parachini, and H.R. Trujillo, 2005, available at www.rand.org/pubs/monographs/MG332/index.html.

- *Local Prosecutors' Response to Terrorism,* Nugent, M.E., J.L. Johnson, B. Bartholomew, and D. Bromirski, April 2005, available at www.ndaa-apri.org/pdf/terrorism_2005.pdf.

- *Methods and Motives: Exploring Links Between Transnational Organized Crime and International Terrorism,* Shelley, L.I., J.T. Picarelli, A. Irby, D.M. Hart, P.A. Craig-Hart, P. Williams, S. Simon, N. Abdullaev, B. Stanislawski, and L. Covill, June 2005, available at www.ncjrs.gov/pdffiles1/nij/grants/211207.pdf.

- "Tracking Modern Day Slavery," *NIJ Journal* 252 (July 2005): 30–31, available at www.ojp.usdoj.gov/nij/journals/252/slavery.html. Also see www.ojp.usdoj.gov/nij/international/global_pub.html.

- *Informal Value Transfer Systems, Terrorism, and Money Laundering,* Passas, N., January 2005, NCJ 208301, available at www.ncjrs.gov/pdffiles1/nij/grants/208301.pdf.

- *Transnational Crime,* Albanese, J., ed. Ontario, Canada: de Sitter Publications, 2005.

Getting the Word Out

One of NIJ's most important missions is to inform. Since 1968, NIJ has published and distributed thousands of publications, developed extensive Web resources, held dozens of national conferences and meetings, and developed and conducted trainings based on emerging discoveries in crime and justice. In FY 2005, NIJ produced more than 30 printed and online publications. These and other products are listed in appendix C.

Electronic media

The Internet is the primary way NIJ disseminates research findings. Downloadable versions of NIJ research reports are available through the National Criminal Justice Reference Service (NCJRS).[74] NIJ submitted 92 final grant reports to NCJRS in FY 2005. NIJ's print publications can also be accessed and downloaded online.[75]

NIJ has been publishing solicitations online for several years. As of October 2005, subscribers to Grants.gov receive automatic e-mail announcements of funding opportunities. Grant awards are also published on the agency's Web site.[76] A searchable grants database that will include links to final reports is under development.

Visits to NIJ's Web site increased 16 percent from 2004 to 2005 (see appendix C, exhibit C-3) and have more than doubled since 2003. Visits to other NIJ-sponsored sites such as JUSTNET increased 32 percent in FY 2005. NIJ plans to restructure its Web site in 2006 to accommodate future growth. Visitors will find a more user-friendly site where they can navigate by topic and find more "new media" products such as Web-only materials and audio and visual files.

Live on the Web. In January 2005, NIJ joined Harvard University's Ash Institute for Democratic Governance and Innovation and the Office of Justice Programs (OJP) to produce a series of live interactive Webcasts. During the first Webcast, "Less-Lethal Force: An Online Session on Emerging Issues and Where to Learn More," OJP's Assistant Attorney General, police officials, and researchers engaged in multimedia presentations and interacted with the online audience.

[74] Access NCJRS at www.ncjrs.gov and search Library/ Abstracts by topic area. Grant reports can also be accessed at http://nij.ncjrs.gov/publications/search_form.asp. Search by a date range or topic area.

[75] Exhibit C-1 in appendix C lists the top 25 publications accessed on the Web in FY 2005.

[76] Online award archives go back to 1995; online solicitation archives go back 2 years.

As part of OJP's coordinated response to Katrina, NIJ sent publications and training materials to help law enforcement officials, forensic laboratory directors, communications technicians, victim service providers, and other responders deal with the aftermath.

JUSTNET

The Justice Technology Information Network (JUSTNET), maintained by the NIJ's National Law Enforcement and Corrections Technology Center (NLECTC), offers information on criminal justice research and development, compliance standards, emerging and promising technologies, and technical assistance and training. It is also a portal to the regional NLECTC offices. Visit JUSTNET at www. justnet.org.

A second Webcast, "DNA in 'Minor' Crimes Yields Major Benefits in Public Safety," discussed how biological evidence obtained from property crime scenes has led to apprehension and conviction of dangerous serial criminals, measurably reducing local property crime losses.[77] This event included a forensics expert from the United Kingdom. Webcasts will continue in 2006.

E-blasts and e-pubs. The Web has become a primary source of current information for citizens and professionals alike. This fact, plus the high cost of printing and distributing publications, has led to a governmentwide trend toward Web-only publications and products that are announced via "e-blasts" to subscribers or targeted e-mail lists. The e-blast describes the product and provides a link to a free downloadable version. This method reaches a wider audience than mailings of printed copies. NIJ routinely sends e-blasts about new publications and events to select audiences and subscribers. For example, a recent e-blast to 100 college newspaper editors announced the release of a Research for Practice summary report on how colleges and universities are reporting and addressing sexual assaults on campus. The editors, in turn, announced the findings to college audiences, thus disseminating the information to thousands more recipients.

Printed copies of new or popular publications and CD–ROMs are still distributed at conferences and mailed to key policymakers, service providers, educators, and other sources. The top 25 printed publications distributed in FY 2005 are listed in appendix C, exhibit C-2.

Conferences and meetings

NIJ sponsored or cosponsored several major national conferences in FY 2005 (see chapter 1). NIJ's annual conference, held in Washington, DC, has been a mainstay for criminal justice professionals for 14 years. The 2005 conference broke attendance records with 1,200 participants attending 50 panels and presentations by nationally and internationally recognized experts. NIJ is expanding the conference for 2006 to encompass a wider audience, thus ensuring that the NIJ Conference remains the premier Federal event for criminal justice professionals.

[77] See *DNA in 'Minor' Crimes Yields Major Benefits in Public Safety,* November 2004, NCJ 207203, available at www. ncjrs.gov/pdffiles1/nij/207203.pdf. Also see chapter 2.

NIJ also sponsors, cosponsors, and participates in many other meetings, seminars, and technical working groups every year, on subjects ranging from terrorism to crime mapping to child safety. Some of these events are discussed throughout this report; most are listed on NIJ's Web site.[78]

Katrina response

As part of OJP's coordinated response to Katrina,[79] NIJ sent publications and training materials to help law enforcement officials, forensic laboratory directors, communications technicians, victim service providers, and other responders deal with the aftermath. NIJ staff also provided support in the field (see chapter 1). Publications dispatched to the field were:

* *Identifying Victims Using DNA: A Guide for Families* (NCJ 209493).

* *Mass Fatality Incidents: A Guide for Human Forensic Identification*, Special Report (NCJ 199758).

* *Lessons Learned From 9/11: DNA Identification in Mass Fatality Incidents*, prepublication draft.[80]

For more information

* NIJ publications, research grant reports, conference proceedings, solicitations, grant award information, and other resources are available at www.ojp.usdoj.gov/nij/welcome.html, or contact: National Institute of Justice, 810 Seventh Street N.W., Washington, DC 20531, 202–307–2942.

* *NIJ Journal*, available at www.ojp.usdoj.gov/nij/journals/welcome.html.

* The National Criminal Justice Reference Service is a federally funded resource for justice information at www.ncjrs.gov, or contact: NCJRS, P.O. Box 6000, Rockville, MD 20849–6000, 800–851–3420 (international callers: 301–519–5500).

[78] Visit www.ojp.usdoj.gov/nij/events/welcome.html.

[79] The other components of OJP are the Bureau of Justice Assistance, Bureau of Justice Statistics, Office of Juvenile Justice and Delinquency Prevention, Office for Victims of Crime, Community Capacity and Development Office, and Office of the Police Corps and Law Enforcement Education.

[80] KADAP is described in chapter 2. The panel's report will be released in 2006 on www.DNA.gov.

Appendixes

'05

Appendix A
Financial Data

Exhibit A-1: NIJ's Research and Development Portfolio, Awards Made FY 1995–2005

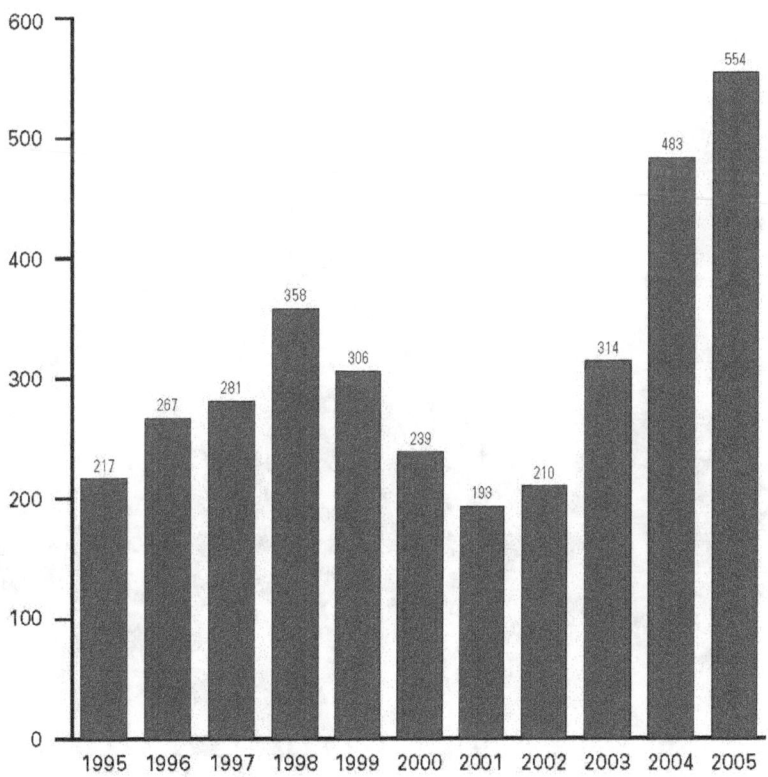

Exhibit A-2: Value of Active Awards, in Millions, FY 1995–2005

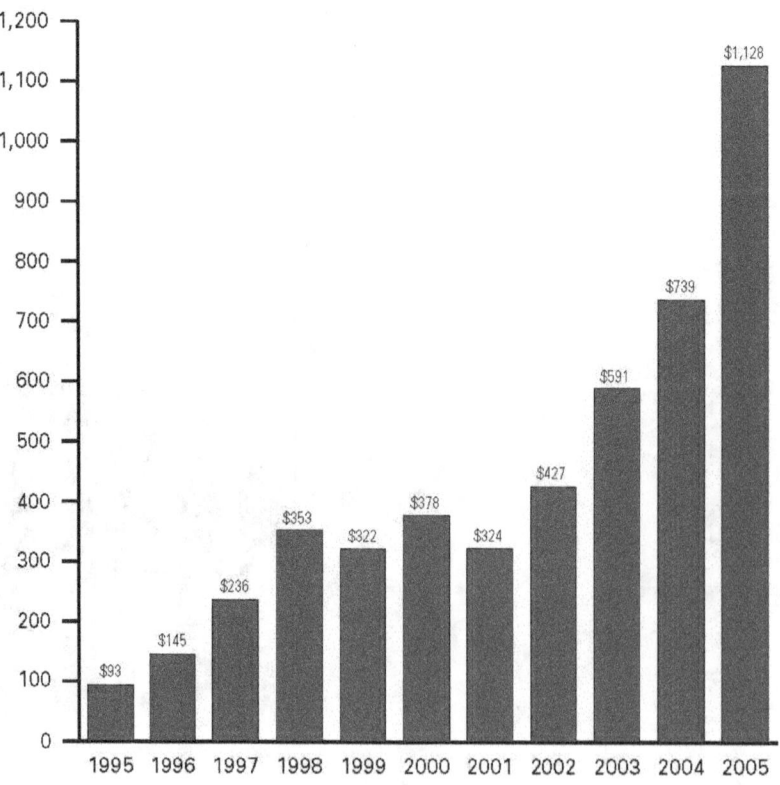

Exhibit A-3: Sources of NIJ Funds, in Millions, FY 1995–2005

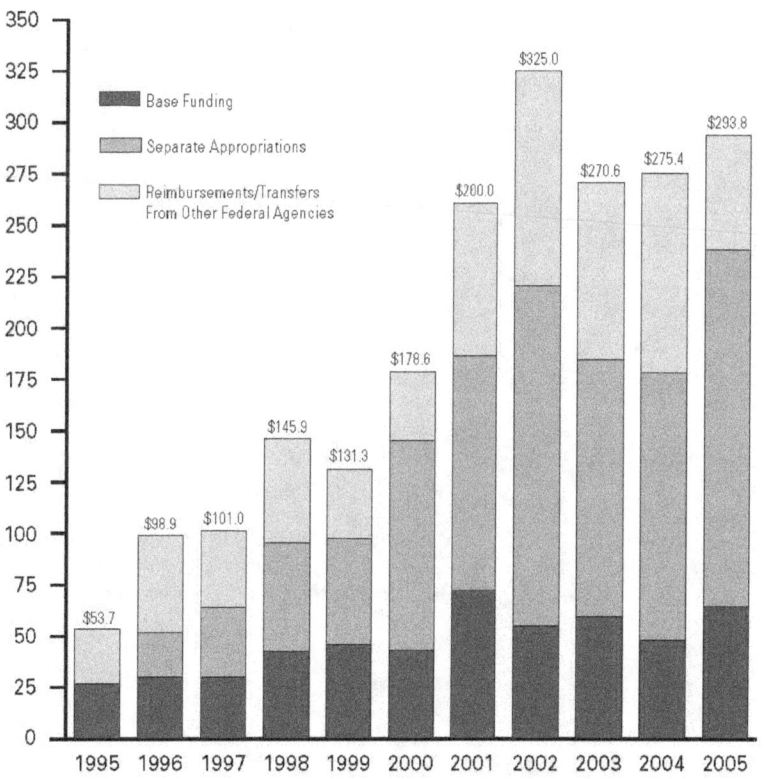

Exhibit A-4: Allocation of NIJ Funds as a Percentage of Total Funding,*
FY 2005

Social Science		
	Research	14%
	Evaluation	3%
Science and Technology		
	Capacity Enhancement**	38%
	Research and Development	21%
	Technology Assistance	9%
	Standards	3%
Program Support		5%
Dissemination		3%
Other		4%

*Total funding of $293.8 million includes NIJ base appropriation of $54.3 million plus separate
 appropriations and funds transfers.

**Grants to improve and enhance crime laboratories.

Exhibit A-5: DNA Funding, FY 2005

The funding request under the President's DNA Initiative was $177 million. Actual funding breakdowns for each purpose area are shown below.

DNA Capacity Enhancement	$39,500,000
DNA Casework Backlog Reduction*	38,500,000
Convicted Offender DNA Backlog Reduction	22,130,752
Training for the Criminal Justice Community	5,000,000
Identifying Missing Persons	3,400,000
Research and Development**	7,000,000
Post-Rescission Total	$108,530,752

*Includes approximately $14.2 million in awards to 38 State and local agencies for solving cold cases.

**$5.6 million reallocated from Capacity Enhancement and $1.4 million reallocated from Missing Persons.

Appendix B
NIJ Awards in FY 2005 (includes first-time awards and supplements to previous awards)

ADMINISTRATIVE SUPPORT

Audit Services for U.S. Crime Laboratories Performing DNA Analysis
National Forensic Science Technology Center
$5,728,286
2004-DN-BX-0079

National Center for Forensic Science Support of Scientific Working Group on Imaging Technology Activities (2006–2007)
University of Central Florida
$125,000
2005-IJ-CX-K021

NIJ Surplus Property Program
Ultimate Enterprises, Ltd.
$123,000
2005-DE-BX-K040

COMMUNICATION AND INFORMATION TECHNOLOGIES

CommTech Program Reviews and Conferencing Activities Support
Aspen Systems Corporation
$130,000
2005-IJ-CX-K108

CommTech Program Support: Subject Matter Expert
Aerospace Corporation
$499,999
2005-IJ-CX-K042

Communication Technology
South Carolina Research Authority
$167,000
2005-IJ-CX-K032

Computer-Assisted Pre-Coordination Resource and Database System, FY 2005 Continuation Program
University of Denver—Colorado Seminary
$374,603
2001-RD-CX-K001

Development of a Comprehensive Suite of New Technology Standards for an Interoperable Communications Network for Land Mobile Communications at the Local, State, and Federal Governmental Levels of Public Safety
Association of Public Safety Communications Officials International, Inc.
$225,000
2005-IJ-CX-K026

Establishing Operational Rules for Law Enforcement and First Responder Tactical Teams Using Ad Hoc Wireless Networks
Drakontas, LLC
$332,571
2005-IJ-CX-K004

Expansion of the CrimeStat Spatial Statistics Program
Ned Levine and Associates
$337,790
2005-IJ-CX-K037

Free Text Conversion and Semantic Analysis
Lehigh University
$100,000
2005-IJ-CX-K005

GPS Public Safety Alert and Notification System
Automated Regional Justice Information System
$200,000
2005-IJ-CX-K022

Information-Led Policing: Random Access to National Law Enforcement Telecommunication System Data (Expansion Pilot)
National Law Enforcement Telecommunication System
$387,400
2005-MU-MU-K019

Link Analysis Survey
Lehigh University
$100,000
2005-IJ-CX-K006

Low-Cost All-Band/All-Mode Radio for Public Safety
Virginia Polytechnic Institute and State University
$399,816
2005-IJ-CX-K018

Prototype Public Safety Cognitive Radio for Universal Interoperability
Virginia Polytechnic Institute and State University
$419,995
2005-IJ-CX-K017

Secure Mobile Broadband Applications
Northrop Grumman IT TASC
$267,054
2005-IJ-CX-K055

Smart Notification as a Tool for Improving and Accelerating DNA-Related Outcomes
New York, City of
$500,000
2005-JP-FX-K011

Steganography Analysis Research Center
DSD Laboratories, Inc.
$493,322
2005-DD-BX-K002

Tactical One-Way Plus Limited Response
Language Translation Headset Demonstration
Integrated Wave Technologies
$93,781
2005–IJ–CX–K053

When Missing Data Are Not Missing: A New
Approach to Evaluating Supplementary
Homicide Reports Imputation Strategies
University of New Mexico
$30,918
2005–IJ–CX–0007

COMPUTER CRIME

Cyber and Electronic Crime Policy Project
National Governors Association
$200,000
2005–DE–BX–K070

Development of an Undercover Multipurpose
Anti-Spoofing Kit
Florida State University
$341,024
2005–MU–MU–K007

Distributed Network Technology for Large-
Scale Code Breaking (The DNA Project)
Florida State University
$149,916
2005–DE–BX–K034

Electronic Crime Partnership Initiative
Robert J. O'Leary
$350,000
2005–DE–BX–K005

Identity Theft: Assessing Offenders' Strategies
and Perceptions of Risk
University of Alabama—Birmingham
$118,167
2005–IJ–CX–0012

Integrity and Authenticity Verification
Algorithms for Digital Photographic Evidence
Polytechnic University
$303,820
2005–IJ–CX–K103

Internet Forensics Toolkit for Law Enforcement
University of California—San Diego
$99,999
2004–MU–MU–K002

Project Who? Geospatial Analysis of
Internet-Related Identity Theft
Elchemy, Inc.
$194,780
2005–IJ–CX–K061

CORRECTIONS

Active RFID (Radio Frequency Identification)
Pilot Program
Los Angeles, County of
$100,000
2005–IJ–CX–K052

Assessing the Validity of Voice Stress Analysis
Tools in a Jail Setting
Oklahoma Department of Mental Health and
Substance Abuse Services
$232,200
2005–IJ–CX–0047

Development and Validation of a Brief Mental
Health Screen for Women in Jail
Policy Research Associates, Inc.
$246,796
2005–IJ–CX–0004

Development of Data-Driven Supervision
Protocols for Positive Parole Outcomes
Georgia State Board of Pardons and Paroles
$272,978
2005–IJ–CX–0029

Impact of Ohio's Progressive Sanction Grid
Ohio Department of Rehabilitation
and Correction
$103,525
2005–IJ–CX–0038

Parole Violations in California: A Multilevel
and Policy-Focused Analysis
University of California
$282,835
2005–IJ–CX–0026

Prison Experience and Reentry: Impact of
Victimization on Coming Home
University of Akron
$466,475
2005–RP–BX–0002

Prisoner Reentry: Impact of Conviction Status
on the Employment Prospects of Young Men
Princeton University
$275,587
2005–IJ–CX–0019

COURTS

Cost Evaluation of Drug Court Programs
Compared to State-Mandated Non-Drug Court
Treatment Programs
Northwest Professional Consortium, Inc.
$284,715
2005–IJ–CX–0010

Judicial Discretion and Sentencing Outcomes:
Incorporating Data From the Courtroom
Wisconsin, State of
$160,079
2005–IJ–CX–0003

MultiState Analysis of Time Consumption
in Capital Appeals
City University of New York
$9,108
2004–IJ–CX–0005

MultiState Analysis of Time Consumption in Capital Appeals, Phase II: State Postconviction Review and Federal Habeas Corpus
City University of New York
$28,978
2004–IJ–CX–0005

National Drug Court Evaluation
Urban Institute
$3,427,055
2003–DC–BX–1001

CRIME LABORATORY IMPROVEMENT

Crime Laboratory Improvement Program
Allegheny, County of
$989,475
2004–LP–CX–K015

Expand Capacity of the Southeast Missouri Regional Crime Lab
Southeast Missouri State University
$493,322
2004–LP–CX–K049

Forensic Science Crime Lab Improvement
Ohio Office of the Attorney General
$246,661
2002–LP–CX–K007

Marshall University Forensic Science Center and Forensic Research Network Initiatives to Improve Forensic Crime Labs
Marshall University
$4,520,121
2005–MU–BX–K020

North Dakota State University Forensic DNA Analysis Laboratory
North Dakota State University
$986,643
2004–RG–CX–K001

Pikes Peak Metro Crime Lab DNA Laboratory
Colorado Springs, City of
$197,329
2004–RC–CX–K019

CRIME PREVENTION

Explaining Developmental Crime Trajectories at Places
University of Maryland
$271,882
2005–IJ–CX–0006

Life Interrupted: Effects of Incarceration on Criminal Trajectories
Urban Institute
$35,000
2005–IJ–CX–0008

Modeling the Dynamics of Street Robberies to Inform Policy and Prevention
Institute for Law and Justice
$141,163
2005–IJ–CX–0015

Preventing Car Crime in Metro's Parking Facilities: A Randomized Clinical Trial
Urban Institute
$207,744
2005–IJ–CX–0034

Project Safe Neighborhoods Academy: Research-Based Training and Technical Assistance to Project Safe Neighborhoods (Year Three Supplement)
Michigan State University
$1,199,998
2002–GP–CX–1003

Situational Violent Crime Prevention at Specific Locations in Community Context: Place and Neighborhood Effects
University of Cincinnati
$187,167
2005–IJ–CX–0030

Social Norms Approach to Community-Based Crime Prevention: Implicit and Explicit Messages on Neighborhood Watch Signs
California State University—San Marcos Foundation
$199,439
2005–IJ–CX–0016

CRIMINAL JUSTICE RESEARCH

Center for Criminal Justice Technology Systems Integration Projects
Mitretek Systems, Inc.
$2,959,930
2001–LT–BX–K002

Committee on Law and Justice
National Academy of Sciences
$250,000
2001–MU–MU–0007

Investigation and Prosecution of Homicide Cases in the United States: The Process of Federal Involvement
National Opinion Research Center
$235,814
2002–IJ–CX–4021

National Clearinghouse for Science, Technology, and the Law
Stetson University, Inc.
$2,959,930
2003–IJ–CX–K024

Reexamination of the Criminal Deterrent
Effects: Capital Punishment and Concealed
Handgun Laws
University of Wisconsin
$32,356
2005–IJ–CX–0020

Simulation Model to Examine the Allocation
of Technology to Improve the Criminal
Justice System
State University of New York
$74,598
2005–IJ–CX–K045

DRUGS AND CRIME

Controlling Methamphetamine Precursors:
From Policy to Practice
Andrews University
$324,764
2005–IJ–CX–0028

Differentiation of MDMA From
Other Methamphetamines of Mass
Spectral Equivalence
Auburn University
$20,000
2005–IJ–CX–K140

Drugs and Crime Research and Evaluation
Abt Associates Inc.
$269,495
2005–IJ–CX–0024

Empirical Investigation of "Going to Scale" in
Drug Interventions
Urban Institute
$196,495
2005–DC–BX–1064

Nontoxic Drug Detection and Identification
Aerosol Technology Program
Mistral Security, Inc.
$739,982
2005–IJ–CX–K023

EDUCATION AND TRAINING

Alternative Modalities for Providing DNA
Training to the Nation's Prosecutors
American Prosecutors Research Institute
$500,000
2004–DN–BX–K017

Conversion of CD–ROM-Based Course: Español
for Law Enforcement V2.0 to the Workforce
Connections Platform
Eastern Kentucky University
$20,000
2005–DE–BX–K072

Institute for Forensic Science: Academic and
Educational Programs Development
Texas Tech University Health Sciences Center
$989,477
2003–IJ–CX–K016

Western Forensic and Law Enforcement
Training Casework Support and Training
Western Forensic Law Enforcement Training
Center at Colorado State University—Pueblo
$98,664
2003–DD–BX–K013

EVALUATION

Evaluation of Active RFID (Radio Frequency
Identification) Pilot Program
RAND Corporation
$150,000
2005–IJ–CX–K062

Evaluation of Multijurisdictional Task Forces,
Phase II: Tool Development and Production
Abt Associates Inc.
$474,435
2005–DD–BX–0002

Evaluation of Office of Juvenile Justice and
Delinquency Prevention FY 2003 Discretionary
Funds Projects
Abt Associates Inc.
$367,960
2005–DD–BX–0037

Evaluation of Office of Juvenile Justice and
Delinquency Prevention FY 2003 Discretionary
Funds Projects
Development Services Group, Inc.
$428,837
2005–MU–MU–0003

Evaluation of the Bureau of Justice
Assistance's Indian Alcohol and Substance
Abuse Demonstration Programs
University of Arizona
$457,200
2005–AC–BX–0011

Evaluation of the Tribal Victim Assistance
Programs at the Lummi Nation and
Passamaquoddy Tribe
American Indian Development Associates
$425,200
2005–VR–GX–0101

Impact and Cost-Benefit Evaluation of the
Oxford House Substance-Free Transitional
Housing Model
Northwest Professional Consortium, Inc.
$662,455
2005–DD–BX–1009

FORENSICS, GENERAL

Forensic Science Initiative
West Virginia University
$4,286,573
2003–RC–CX–K001

National Center for Forensic Science
University of Central Florida
$928,984
2005–MU–MU–K044

Scientific Working Group on Dog and Orthogonal Detectors
Florida International University
$97,019
2005–IJ–CX–K031

FORENSICS, RESEARCH AND DEVELOPMENT

Adding Human Expertise to the Quantitative Analysis of Fingerprints
Indiana University
$431,255
2005–MU–BX–K076

Analysis of Level III Characteristics at High Resolutions
International Biometric Group, LLC
$461,495
2005–MU–MU–K063

Continued Development of Capillary Electrophoresis Microdevice for Forensic DNA Analysis
National Institute of Standards and Technology
$800,707
2003–IJ–R–029

DNA Quantitation, STR Microvariant Allele Sequencing, STRBase Updates, and SNP and STR Multiplexing Project
National Institute of Standards and Technology
$1,212,127
2003–IJ–R–029

Elemental Analysis of Glass and Paint Materials by Laser Ablation Inductively Coupled Plasma Mass Spectrometry for Forensic Application
Florida International University
$30,002
2003–IJ–CX–K004

Elemental Analysis of Glass by Scanning Electron Microscopy-Energy Dispersive Spectroscopy, X-Ray Fluorescence, Electron Probe Micro Analysis, Laser-Induced Breakdown Spectroscopy, and Laser Ablation Inductively Coupled Plasma Mass Spectrometry
Florida International University
$292,149
2005–IJ–CX–K069

Enhanced Forensic Mass Spectrometry Methods
West Virginia University
$169,091
2005–IJ–CX–K014

Enhancing the Size, Sampling, and Quality of Forensic mtDNA Databases
Armed Forces Institute of Pathology
$1,891,390
2005–DN–R–086

Evaluation of Ultraviolet Radiation Absorbing Compounds in Textile Fibers Using High-Performance Liquid Chromatography and Atmospheric Pressure Ionization Mass Spectrometry
Sacramento, County of
$31,151
2005–IJ–CX–K008

Friction Ridge Analysis Research
Ultra Scan Corporation
$126,601
2005–DD–BX–K056

Geometric Morphometric Tools for the Classification of Human Skulls
North Carolina State University
$199,635
2005–MU–BX–K078

Improving Methods for Fingerprint Development on Handguns
Technical Support Working Group
$70,000
2005–IF–R–051

Instrumental Analysis of Pigmented Ink Jet Printer Inks
Indiana University
$261,258
2005–IJ–CX–K064

Knife and Saw Tool Mark Analysis in Bone: Interpreting Criminal Mutilation and Dismemberment
Mercyhurst College
$201,853
2005–IJ–CX–K016

Latent-Print Detection by Macro-Raman Imaging
Department of Energy: Oak Ridge National Laboratory
$299,000
2005–DN–R–094

Measuring Atomic Bomb-Derived ^{14}C Levels in Human Remains to Determine Year of Birth and/or Year of Death
University of Arizona
$147,391
2005–IJ–CX–K013

Quantitative Assessment of the Individuality of Friction Ridge Patterns
State University of New York
$596,478
2005–DD–BX–K012

The Development of a Method for Objective Physical Matching: Meeting Daubert
Technical Support Working Group
$25,000
2005–IF–R–051

FORENSICS AND INVESTIGATIVE SCIENCES

DNA Capacity Enhancement Program Formula Grants

Alabama Department of Forensic Sciences
$555,601
2005–DA–BX–K004

Alameda County Sheriff's Office
$93,201
2005–DA–BX–K031

Albuquerque, City of
$121,932
2005–DA–BX–K015

Allegheny County Forensic Lab Division of Coroner's Office
$101,627
2005–DA–BX–K110

Anne Arundel, County of
$45,980
2005–DA–BX–K005

Arizona Criminal Justice Commission
$387,065
2005–DA–BX–K006

Arizona Department of Public Safety
$265,728
2005–DA–BX–K007

Arkansas State Crime Laboratory
$306,072
2005–DA–BX–K103

Austin, City of
$112,809
2005–DA–BX–K016

Baltimore, City of
$171,743
2005–DA–BX–K017

Baltimore, County of
$89,212
2005–DA–BX–K008

Bexar, County of
$199,051
2005–DA–BX–K032

Broward County Sheriff's Office
$154,655
2005–DA–BX–K010

California Department of Justice
$751,737
2005–DA–BX–K011

Charlotte-Mecklenburg Police Department
$52,539
2005–DA–BX–K018

Colorado Department of Public Safety
$482,392
2005–DA–BX–K027

Columbus, City of
$100,000
2005–DA–BX–K019

Connecticut Department of Public Safety
$181,600
2005–DA–BX–K043

Connecticut Department of Public Safety
$214,851
2005–DA–BX–K044

Contra Costa, County of
$94,807
2005–DA–BX–K030

Cuyahoga County Coroner's Office
$170,019
2005–DA–BX–K040

Dallas, County of
$372,193
2005–DA–BX–K042

Delaware Health and Social Services
$107,141
2005–DA–BX–K041

Denver, City and County of
$105,891
2005–DA–BX–K012

Detroit, City of
$335,414
2005–DA–BX–K020

District of Columbia Metropolitan
Police Department
$148,634
2005-DA-BX-K045

DuPage County Sheriff's Department
$43,166
2005-DA-BX-K046

Erie, County of
$130,479
2005-DA-BX-K033

Florida Department of Law Enforcement
$1,541,793
2005-DA-BX-K047

Fresno County Sheriff's Department
$70,000
2005-DA-BX-K048

Georgia Bureau of Investigation
$821,039
2005-DA-BX-K049

Hamilton County Administration
$149,981
2005-DA-BX-K050

Harris, County of
$219,322
2005-DA-BX-K051

Honolulu Police Department
$110,552
2005-DA-BX-K013

Houston, City of
$277,030
2005-DA-BX-K021

Idaho State Police
$111,280
2005-DA-BX-K052

Illinois State Police
$1,309,335
2005-DA-BX-K053

Indiana State Police
$585,725
2005-DA-BX-K054

Instituto de Ciencias Forenses de Puerto Rico
$279,234
2005-DA-BX-K055

Iowa Department of Public Safety
$183,400
2005-DA-BX-K088

Johnson County Board of Commissioners
$66,135
2005-DA-BX-K056

Kansas Bureau of Investigation
$210,000
2005-DA-BX-K057

Kansas City Police Department
$191,928
2005-DA-BX-K009

Kentucky State Police
$352,970
2005-DA-BX-K028

Kern County District Attorney
$71,352
2005-DA-BX-K034

Las Vegas Metropolitan Police Department
$340,360
2005-DA-BX-K058

Los Angeles, City of
$687,975
2005-DA-BX-K022

Los Angeles County Sheriff's Department
$593,232
2005-DA-BX-K035

Louisiana State Police
$692,014
2005-DA-BX-K106

Maine Department of Public Safety
$105,152
2005-DA-BX-K060

Mansfield, City of
$135,000
2005-DA-BX-K023

Maryland State Police
$163,228
2005-DA-BX-K061

Massachusetts State Police
$515,000
2005-DA-BX-K062

Miami-Dade, County of
$325,815
2005-DA-BX-K063

Michigan State Police
$1,389,080
2005-DA-BX-K089

Mississippi Department of Public Safety
$382,242
2005-DA-BX-K107

Missouri Southern State University
$24,171
2005-DA-BX-K059

Missouri State Highway Patrol
$119,775
2005-DA-BX-K064

Montana Department of Justice
$78,034
2005-DA-BX-K105

Montgomery County Department of Police
$64,976
2005-DA-BX-K065

Montgomery, County of
$443,476
2005–DA–BX–K066

Nebraska State Patrol
$156,591
2005–DA–BX–K067

New Hampshire Department of Safety
$79,046
2005–DA–BX–K068

New Jersey Department of Law and
Public Safety
$492,225
2005–DA–BX–K079

New Mexico Department of Public Safety
$176,188
2005–DA–BX–K090

New York State Division of Criminal
Justice Services
$1,207,226
2005–DA–BX–K069

North Carolina Department of Crime Control
and Public Safety
$639,666
2005–DA–BX–K070

North Dakota Office of the Attorney General
$46,324
2005–DA–BX–K071

Northern Illinois Police Crime Laboratory
$48,058
2005–DA–BX–K072

Oakland Police Department
$83,904
2005–DA–BX–K024

Ohio Office of the Attorney General
$453,476
2005–DA–BX–K091

Oklahoma City
$87,332
2005–DA–BX–K025

Oklahoma State Bureau of Investigation
$397,788
2005–DA–BX–K074

Orange County Sheriff—Coroner Department
$226,674
2004–DN–BX–4069

Orange County Sheriff—Coroner Department
$164,395
2005–DA–BX–K036

Oregon State Police
$365,474
2005–DA–BX–K092

Palm Beach County Sheriff's Office
$152,103
2005–DA–BX–K075

Pennsylvania State Police
$711,386
2005–DA–BX–K076

Philadelphia Police Department
$382,594
2005–DA–BX–K104

Rhode Island Department of Health, Division
of Laboratories
$150,539
2005–DA–BX–K077

Richland, County of
$97,445
2005–DA–BX–K078

Sacramento County District Attorney
$157,663
2005–DA–BX–K080

San Bernardino, County of
$189,093
2005–DA–BX–K037

San Diego, City of
$135,732
2005–DA–BX–K026

San Diego, County of
$130,049
2005–DA–BX–K081

San Francisco City and County
Police Department
$89,371
2005–DA–BX–K014

San Mateo County Sheriff's Office
$40,017
2005–DA–BX–K082

Santa Clara, County of
$96,492
2005–DA–BX–K038

Sedgwick, County of
$54,075
2005–DA–BX–K083

South Carolina Law Enforcement Division
$511,584
2005–DA–BX–K084

South Dakota Office of the Attorney General
$103,517
2005–DA–BX–K073

Southeast Missouri State University
$18,399
2005–DA–BX–K108

St. Charles, County of
$17,317
2005–DA–BX–K085

St. Louis, County of
$53,033
2005-DA-BX-K086

St. Louis Metropolitan Police Department
$53,393
2005-DA-BX-K087

Tennessee Bureau of Investigation
$445,803
2005-DA-BX-K093

Texas Department of Public Safety
$1,215,071
2005-DA-BX-K094

Utah Department of Public Safety
$269,985
2005-DA-BX-K111

Ventura, County of
$38,554
2005-DA-BX-K039

Vermont Department of Public Safety
$38,366
2005-DA-BX-K096

Virginia Department of Criminal Justice Services
$621,250
2005-DA-BX-K029

Washington State Patrol
$866,226
2005-DA-BX-K097

West Virginia State Police
$102,026
2005-DA-BX-K098

Wisconsin Department of Justice
$391,905
2005-DA-BX-K109

Wyoming Office of the Attorney General
$42,629
2005-DA-BX-K099

DNA, Missing Persons

**Developing Improved Capacity for Texas
Missing Persons Cases and Fort Worth Area
Casework in Sexual Assault and Homicide**
University of North Texas Health Science
Center—Fort Worth
$283,868
2005-DA-BX-K095

**Perform Anthropological, mtDNA, and STR
Analysis of Unidentified Human Remains and
Family Reference Samples for Entry**
University of North Texas Health Science
Center—Fort Worth
$1,484,782
2004-DN-BX-K212

DNA, Research and Development

**Determination of the Age (Time Since
Deposition) of a Biological Stain**
University of Central Florida
$124,753
2005-MU-BX-K071

**Determination of the Physical Characteristics
of an Individual From Biological Stains**
University of Central Florida
$224,776
2005-MU-BX-K075

**Development and Evaluation of a Whole
Genome Amplification Method for Accurate
Multiplex STR Genotyping of Compromised
Forensic Casework Samples**
Virginia Commonwealth University
$225,616
2005-DA-BX-K002

**Development of a Procedure for
Dielectrophoretic Separation of Sperm and
Epithelial Cells for Application to Sexual
Assault Case Evidence**
California Department of Justice
$205,407
2005-DA-BX-K001

**Development of Multiplex PCR and Linear
Array Probe Assay Targeting Informative
Polymorphisms Within the Entire
Mitochondrial Genome**
Children's Hospital
Oakland Research Institute
$469,123
2005-MU-BX-K074

**DNA-Based Identification of Forensically
Important Diptera**
University of Cincinnati
$574,557
2005-DA-BX-K102

**Electro-Elution Assisted Purification of DNA
for Forensic Analysis**
University of Virginia
$20,000
2005-DA-BX-K100

Gene Polymorphism and Human Pigmentation
University of Arizona
$184,105
2002-IJ-CX-K010

**Improving the Efficiency of DNA Casework
Analysis Through Simple, Effective,
PCR-Based Screening Methods**
Vermont Department of Public Safety
$256,000
2005-DA-BX-K003

Mitochondrial DNA Mixture Separation and Analysis by Denaturing High-Performance Chromatography
University of Denver
$254,549
2003-IJ-CX-K104

Nanotechnology DNA Sequencing: Improving DNA Processing Technologies
Brown University
$542,654
2004-LT-BX-K001

SNP-Based Microarray Technology for Use in Forensic Applications
Affymetrix, Inc.
$638,098
2005-DA-BX-K101

Use of Mini-STRs as Tools for the Investigation of DNA Degradation and Inhibition
Florida International University
$171,394
2005-MU-BX-K073

DNA, Solving Cold Cases

Alabama, State of
$136,947
2005-DN-BX-K005

Alameda County Sheriff's Office
$430,434
2005-DN-BX-K007

Albuquerque, City of
$75,014
2005-DN-BX-K014

Arizona Department of Public Safety
$799,583
2005-DN-BX-K018

Burlingame, City of
$11,365
2005-DN-BX-K038

Connecticut Division of Criminal Justice
$205,701
2005-DN-BX-K025

Fort Lauderdale, City of
$435,961
2005-DN-BX-K022

Fresno, City of
$1,224,751
2005-DN-BX-K006

Fulton County District Attorney's Office
$714,150
2005-DN-BX-K017

Hawaii, State of
$790,276
2005-DN-BX-K026

Hayward, City of
$419,017
2005-DN-BX-K033

Houston, City of
$179,364
2005-DN-BX-K035

Indiana State Police
$728,970
2005-DN-BX-K028

Joliet, City of
$455,301
2005-DN-BX-K008

Kansas Bureau of Investigation
$342,060
2005-DN-BX-K013

Los Angeles, County of
$882,399
2005-DN-BX-K019

Maine Department of Public Safety
$250,349
2005-DN-BX-K024

Maryland State Police
$600,624
2005-DN-BX-K037

Massachusetts State Police
$500,000
2005-DN-BX-K020

Montgomery, County of
$171,159
2005-DN-BX-K021

Muncie, City of
$60,500
2005-DN-BX-K036

Nebraska State Patrol
$226,098
2005-DN-BX-K010

North Little Rock, City of
$48,175
2005-DN-BX-K015

North Miami, City of
$525,815
2005-DN-BX-K012

North Miami Beach, City of
$106,743
2005-DN-BX-K023

Ohio Attorney General Bureau of Criminal Identification and Investigation
$661,878
2005-DN-BX-K002

Orange County Sheriff—Coroner Department
$352,480
2005-DN-BX-K016

Palm Beach County Sheriff's Office
$374,761
2005-DN-BX-K031

Pima County Sheriff's Department
$363,751
2005-DN-BX-K009

Sacramento, City of
$532,832
2005–DN–BX–K030

San Diego, County of
$472,554
2005–DN–BX–K034

Shreveport, City of
$263,200
2005–DN–BX–K029

South Dakota Office of the Attorney General
$233,559
2005–DN–BX–K032

Spartanburg, City of
$196,112
2005–DN–BX–K001

St. Louis, County of
$97,385
2005–DN–BX–K027

Ventura, County of
$188,264
2005–DN–BX–K003

Westchester, County of
$64,929
2005–DN–BX–K004

Wisconsin Department of Justice
$122,692
2005–DN–BX–K011

*Forensic Casework DNA Backlog
Reduction Program Formula Grants*

Alabama Department of Forensic Sciences
$863,280
2005–DN–BX–K040

Alabama Department of Forensic Sciences
$482,225
2005–DN–BX–K053

Alameda County Sheriff's Office
$77,215
2005–DN–BX–K072

Allegheny County Coroner's Office
Forensic Lab Division
$67,775
2005–DN–BX–K054

Arizona Criminal Justice Commission
$329,164
2005–DN–BX–K055

Arizona Department of Public Safety
$229,164
2005–DN–BX–K056

Arkansas State Crime Laboratory
$265,655
2005–DN–BX–K057

Austin, City of
$99,992
2005–DN–BX–K118

Boston, City of
$115,104
2005–DN–BX–K063

Broward County Sheriff's Office
$134,163
2005–DN–BX–K059

California Department of Justice
$756,927
2005–DN–BX–K041

California Department of Justice
$622,144
2005–DN–BX–K060

Charlotte, City of
$40,000
2005–DN–BX–K064

Colorado Department of Public Safety
$161,953
2005–DN–BX–K119

Connecticut Department of Public Safety
$143,284
2005–DN–BX–K079

Contra Costa, County of
$52,620
2005–DN–BX–K071

Cuyahoga County Coroner's Office
$134,548
2005–DN–BX–K076

Dallas, County of
$288,660
2005–DN–BX–K121

Delaware Health and Social Services
$42,494
2005–DN–BX–K043

Delaware Health and Social Services
$58,821
2005–DN–BX–K077

Denver, City and County of
$53,356
2005–DN–BX–K061

Erie, County of
$30,727
2005–DN–BX–K120

Florida Department of Law Enforcement
$1,338,036
2005–DN–BX–K080

Fresno County Sheriff's Department
$40,000
2005–DN–BX–K081

Georgia Bureau of Investigation
$200,000
2005–DN–BX–K044

Harris, County of
$399,379
2005–DN–BX–K122

Illinois State Police
$80,094
2005–DN–BX–K045

Illinois State Police
$1,175,886
2005–DN–BX–K123

Indiana State Police
$508,371
2005–DN–BX–K082

Kansas Bureau of Investigation
$227,213
2005–DN–BX–K046

Kansas Bureau of Investigation
$111,580
2005–DN–BX–K083

Kansas City Board of Police Commissioners
$190,445
2005–DN–BX–K058

Kentucky State Police
$53,313
2005–DN–BX–K042

Kentucky State Police
$306,134
2005–DN–BX–K069

Las Vegas Metropolitan Police Department
$118,800
2005–DN–BX–K052

Las Vegas Metropolitan Police Department
$263,185
2005–DN–BX–K084

Los Angeles, City of
$126,800
2005–DN–BX–K065

Los Angeles, County of
$242,321
2005–DN–BX–K073

Louisiana State Police
$600,623
2005–DN–BX–K085

Maine Department of Public Safety
$91,188
2005–DN–BX–K086

Massachusetts State Police
$287,425
2005–DN–BX–K087

Miami-Dade, County of
$282,756
2005–DN–BX–K088

Michigan State Police
$1,496,748
2005–DN–BX–K106

Mississippi Department of Public Safety
$331,761
2005–DN–BX–K089

Missouri State Highway Patrol
$266,998
2005–DN–BX–K039

Missouri State Highway Patrol
$118,846
2005–DN–BX–K090

Montana Department of Justice
$68,079
2005–DN–BX–K078

Montgomery, County of
$223,548
2005–DN–BX–K091

Nebraska State Patrol
$135,911
2005–DN–BX–K092

New Hampshire Department of Safety
$61,576
2005–DN–BX–K093

New Jersey Department of Law and
Public Safety
$1,375,407
2005–DN–BX–K051

New Jersey Department of Law and
Public Safety
$314,715
2005–DN–BX–K094

New York State Division of Criminal
Justice Services
$237,000
2005–DN–BX–K047

New York State Division of Criminal
Justice Services
$369,240
2005–DN–BX–K124

North Carolina Department of Crime Control
and Public Safety
$426,593
2005–DN–BX–K095

North Dakota, State of
$40,206
2005–DN–BX–K096

Northern Illinois Police Crime Laboratory
$69,602
2005–DN–BX–K097

Oakland, City of
$69,524
2005–DN–BX–K066

Ohio Office of the Attorney General
$739,534
2005–DN–BX–K107

Orange County Sheriff—Coroner Department
$173,440
2004–DN–BX–4141

Palm Beach County Sheriff's Office
$118,830
2005–DN–BX–K099

Pennsylvania State Police
$136,308
2005–DN–BX–K100

Philadelphia Police Department
$277,116
2005–DN–BX–K067

Rhode Island Department of Health
$130,732
2005–DN–BX–K101

San Diego, City of
$112,236
2005–DN–BX–K068

San Diego, County of
$115,100
2005–DN–BX–K125

San Francisco City and County
Police Department
$73,529
2005–DN–BX–K062

San Mateo County Sheriff's Office
$33,212
2005–DN–BX–K102

Santa Clara, County of
$79,937
2005–DN–BX–K074

South Carolina Law Enforcement Division
$528,597
2005–DN–BX–K103

South Dakota Office of the Attorney General
$89,840
2005–DN–BX–K098

St. Louis, County of
$52,621
2005–DN–BX–K104

St. Louis Metropolitan Police Department
$52,973
2005–DN–BX–K113

Tarrant, County of
$168,700
2005–DN–BX–K126

Tennessee Bureau of Investigation
$470,033
2005–DN–BX–K108

Texas, State of
$419,391
2005–DN–BX–K048

University of North Texas Health Science
Center—Fort Worth
$561,747
2005–DN–BX–K127

Ventura, County of
$32,000
2005–DN–BX–K075

Vermont Department of Public Safety
$39,566
2005–DN–BX–K049

Vermont Department of Public Safety
$33,299
2005–DN–BX–K109

Virginia Department of Criminal Justice Services
$539,204
2005–DN–BX–K070

Washington State Patrol
$223,866
2005–DN–BX–K110

Washoe County Sheriff's Department
$66,227
2005–DN–BX–K050

West Virginia Division of Public Safety
$88,552
2005–DN–BX–K111

Wisconsin Department of Justice
$314,135
2005–DN–BX–K128

Wyoming Office of the Attorney General
$28,429
2005–DN–BX–K112

*Paul Coverdell Forensic Science
Improvement Grants*

Alabama Department of Economic and
Community Affairs
$146,930
2005–DN–BX–0115

Alaska Department of Public Safety
$82,639
2005–DN–BX–0001

Anchorage, Municipality of
$95,000
2005–DN–BX–0002

Arizona Criminal Justice Commission
$281,293
2005–DN–BX–0004

Arkansas Department of Finance
and Administration
$89,278
2005–DN–BX–0003

Avondale, City of
$84,116
2005–DN–BX–0121

California Governor's Office of
Emergency Services
$1,164,088
2005–DN–BX–0110

Carbondale, City of
$65,403
2005–DN–BX–0007

Chandler Police Department
$22,306
2005-DN-BX-0112

Colorado Division of Criminal Justice
$149,240
2005-DN-BX-0101

Columbia, City of
$92,501
2005-DN-BX-0072

Columbus, City of
$89,985
2005-DN-BX-0075

Connecticut, State of
$113,634
2005-DN-BX-0062

Dallas, City of
$95,000
2005-DN-BX-0128

Dallas, County of
$95,000
2005-DN-BX-0016

Delaware Criminal Justice Council
$82,639
2005-DN-BX-0093

Denver, City and County of
$57,305
2005-DN-BX-0079

District of Columbia Justice
Grants Administration
$82,639
2005-DN-BX-0081

Douglas County Government
$94,988
2005-DN-BX-0092

Douglas, County of
$91,810
2005-DN-BX-0013

Eau Claire, City of
$18,000
2005-DN-BX-0026

Florida Department of Law Enforcement
$564,253
2005-DN-BX-0073

Fort Worth, City of
$95,000
2005-DN-BX-0088

Fulton County Medical Examiner
$80,233
2004-DN-BX-4184

Georgia Criminal Justice Coordinating Council
$286,369
2005-DN-BX-0127

Grand Rapids, City of
$45,420
2005-DN-BX-0096

Hamilton County Administration
$79,175
2004-DN-BX-4210

Harris, County of
$95,000
2005-DN-BX-0017

Idaho State Police
$82,639
2005-DN-BX-0048

Illinois Criminal Justice Information Authority
$412,349
2005-DN-BX-0080

Indiana Criminal Justice Institute
$202,307
2005-DN-BX-0094

Indianapolis-Marion County Forensic
Services Agency
$36,410
2005-DN-BX-0077

Instituto de Ciencias Forenses de Puerto Rico
$178,802
2005-DN-BX-0104

Iowa Governor's Office of Drug Control Policy
$95,823
2005-DN-BX-0006

Kansas City Police Department
$94,624
2005-DN-BX-0078

Kansas Criminal Justice Coordinating Council
$88,722
2005-DN-BX-0113

Kentucky Justice and Public Safety Cabinet
$134,467
2005-DN-BX-0076

King County Sheriff's Office
$30,516
2005-DN-BX-0116

Las Vegas Metropolitan Police Department
$95,000
2005-DN-BX-0068

Long Beach, City of
$95,000
2005-DN-BX-0005

Long Branch, City of
$69,650
2005-DN-BX-0107

Louisiana Commission on Law Enforcement
and Administration of Justice
$146,463
2005-DN-BX-0051

Maryland Governor's Office of Crime Control
and Prevention
$180,268
2005–DN–BX–0091

Massachusetts State Police
$208,110
2005–DN–BX–0069

Miami Police Department
$95,000
2005–DN–BX–0123

Michigan Office of Drug Control Policy
$230,328
2004–DN–BX–4155

Michigan Office of Drug Control Policy
$327,989
2005–DN–BX–0085

Minneapolis, City of
$55,918
2005–DN–BX–0084

Minnesota Department of Public Safety
$165,442
2005–DN–BX–0070

Mississippi Division of Public Safety Planning
$189,154
2005–DN–BX–0009

Missouri Department of Public Safety
$186,643
2005–DN–BX–0008

Monroe, County of
$65,495
2005–DN–BX–0014

Montana Board of Crime Control
$82,639
2005–DN–BX–0010

Nebraska State Patrol
$82,639
2005–DN–BX–0097

Nevada Department of Public Safety
$82,639
2005–DN–BX–0054

New Hampshire Department of Justice
$140,051
2005–DN–BX–0083

New Jersey Department of Law and
Public Safety
$282,136
2005–DN–BX–0114

New Mexico Department of Public Safety
$82,639
2005–DN–BX–0100

New York State Division of Criminal
Justice Services
$623,604
2005–DN–BX–0089

North Carolina Department of Crime Control
and Public Safety
$277,023
2005–DN–BX–0011

North Dakota Office of the Attorney General
$82,639
2005–DN–BX–0012

Ohio Office of Criminal Justice Services
$371,657
2005–DN–BX–0058

Oklahoma District Attorney's Council
$114,282
2005–DN–BX–0105

Onondaga County Health Department
$50,720
2005–DN–BX–0124

Orange County Sheriff—Coroner Department
$80,233
2004–DN–BX–4178

Oregon State Police
$116,585
2005–DN–BX–0098

Oxford Police Department
$38,250
2005–DN–BX–0129

Pennsylvania Commission on Crime
and Delinquency
$402,381
2005–DN–BX–0126

Rhode Island Justice Commission
$82,639
2005–DN–BX–0066

Riverside, City of
$95,000
2005–DN–BX–0119

Rogers, City of
$28,191
2005–DN–BX–0120

San Diego, County of
$79,537
2005–DN–BX–0130

San Francisco, City and County of
$74,300
2005–DN–BX–0099

Santa Ana, City of
$48,188
2005–DN–BX–0111

Sedgwick, County of
$58,250
2005–DN–BX–0109

South Carolina Department of Public Safety
$136,158
2005–DN–BX–0122

South Dakota Office of the Attorney General
$121,725
2005–DN–BX–0086

St. Joseph County Prosecutor's Office
$87,850
2005–DN–BX–0061

St. Louis, City of
$95,000
2005–DN–BX–0108

St. Lucie County Sheriff's Office
$85,500
2005–DN–BX–0131

Summit, County of
$56,600
2005–DN–BX–0082

Tennessee, State of
$191,389
2005–DN–BX–0015

Texas Office of the Governor
$729,432
2005–DN–BX–0103

Utah, County of
$94,307
2005–DN–BX–0090

Utah Department of Public Safety
$82,824
2005–DN–BX–0064

Ventura, County of
$95,000
2005–DN–BX–0074

Vermont Department of Public Safety
$82,639
2005–DN–BX–0065

Virginia Department of Health
$241,949
2005–DN–BX–0067

Waco, City of
$72,486
2005–DN–BX–0117

Washington, State of
$201,211
2005–DN–BX–0018

West Virginia Division of Criminal
Justice Services
$82,639
2005–DN–BX–0087

Westminster, City of
$76,134
2005–DN–BX–0071

Whitley County Coroner's Office
$60,068
2005–DN–BX–0095

Winnebago, County of
$40,967
2005–DN–BX–0118

Wisconsin Department of Justice
$178,678
2005–DN–BX–0019

Wyoming Office of the Attorney General
$82,639
2005–DN–BX–0020

LESS-LETHAL INCAPACITATION

**Analysis of Human Injuries and Taser
Deployment: Effect of Less-Lethal Weapons in
the De-escalation of Force**
Florida Gulf Coast University
$99,856
2005–IJ–CX–K050

**Analysis of Less-Lethal Technologies: Taser
Versus Stinger**
Florida Gulf Coast University
$36,103
2005–IJ–CX–K049

**Collection and Dissemination of Applicable
Databases to the Law Enforcement
Community: Phases II and III**
Pennsylvania State University
$250,000
2004–IJ–CX–K039

**Effect of Taser on Cardiac, Respiratory, and
Metabolic Physiology in Human Subjects**
University of California—San Diego
$231,754
2005–IJ–CX–K051

**Evaluation of Standard Development for
Kinetic Energy Impact Munitions**
Wayne State University
$149,493
2002–MU–CX–K006

**Human Electromuscular Incapacitation
Devices in Trainees**
New Jersey Medical School—Medicine and
Dentistry
$375,000
2005–IJ–CX–K065

**Interdisciplinary Working Group for Review of
Kinetic Energy Impact Injuries**
Wayne State University
$190,246
2005–MU–MU–K001

**Less-Lethal Weapon Technology Review and
Operational Needs**
Pennsylvania State University
$300,000
2004–IJ–CX–K040

POLICING

Assessing Police Use of Force Policy and Outcomes
Michigan State University
$376,255
2005–IJ–CX–0055

Cost-Effective and High-Performance Submicron Ceramic Armor
Materials Modification, Inc.
$252,924
2005–MU–MU–K054

Determining an Optimal Police Search Area for a Serial Criminal
Towson University
$24,995
2005–IJ–CX–K036

Enhancing Local and State Law Enforcement's Understanding and Use of Emerging Technology
International Association of Chiefs of Police
$274,875
2005–DE–BX–K001

Evaluation of Police Use of Force Outcomes
University of South Carolina
Research Foundation
$647,387
2005–IJ–CX–0056

Impact of Law Enforcement Shift Practices and Extra-Duty Employment on Various Health, Safety, Performance, and Quality-of-Life Measures
Police Foundation
$998,870
2005–FS–BX–0057

Shifts, Extended Work Hours, and Fatigue: Assessment of Health and Personal Risks for Police Officers
State University of New York
$501,676
2005–FS–BX–0004

Technology Improvement Project for the Middle Rio Grande Region of Texas, Phase II
Middle Rio Grande Development Council
$1,973,000
2004–LT–BX–K003

Unresolved Problems and Powerful Potentials: Improving Partnerships Between Law Enforcement Leaders and University-Based Researchers, Phase II
International Association of Chiefs of Police
$49,997
2005–IJ–CX–0060

SCHOOLS

Communications Technology, Technical Support, Outreach, and School Safety
Sheriffs Association of Texas
$1,025,000
2005–MU–MU–K033

SENSORS AND SURVEILLANCE

Apparatus for Enhanced Deception Detection
Authenti-Corporation
$437,592
2005–IJ–CX–K066

Center for Advanced Biometric Research and Evaluation
University of Notre Dame du Lac
$246,661
2005–DD–CX–K078

Efficient, Field-Optimized, Multimodal Biometric System
International Biometric Group, LLC
$431,556
2005–IJ–CX–K059

Facenorm: Normalization Plug-In for Improved Face Recognition of Noncooperative Individuals
Carnegie Mellon University
$496,737
2005–IJ–CX–K057

Fast Capture Fingerprint and Palm Print Technology
Smiths Detection, Inc.
$1,800,597
2005–IJ–CX–K067

Fast Fingerprint Capture Technology to Capture Up to 10 Roll-Equivalent Fingerprints Within 15 Seconds
TBS North America, Inc.
$1,448,788
2005–IJ–CX–K071

Handshot ID: A Fast 3-D Imaging System for Capturing Fingerprints, Palm Prints, and Hand Geometry
Carnegie Mellon University
$773,341
2005–IJ–CX–K046

High-Quality 3-D Facial Images From Surveillance Video
General Electric
$499,962
2005–IJ–CX–K060

License Plate Reader Evaluation Project
G2Tactics
$100,000
2004–IJ–CX–K016

Sensor, Surveillance, and Biometrics
Technologies for Criminal Justice
BRTRC, Inc.
$93,235
2005–IJ–CX–K058

TECHNOLOGY

Backscatter and High-Energy Transmission
X-Ray Technology
South Carolina Research Authority
$3,946,573
2002–MU–MU–K011

Northeast Technology and Product
Assessment Committee
Massachusetts Department of Correction
$50,000
2004–LT–BX–K086

Solid-State Radio Frequency Directed Energy
(RFDE LL) Tabletop Demonstrator and
Oscillator Devices Integration With Solid-State
RFDE Arrays
Raytheon Company
$249,995
2004–IJ–CX–K035

Pursuit Management Technology

Engine Stopping Using Intelligent Waveform
Modulation
Fiore Industries, Inc.
$340,505
2005–DE–BX–K029

Road Sentry Optimization for Deployment
Boyer & Associates
$100,000
2005–IJ–CX–K025

*Technology, National Law Enforcement
and Corrections Technology Centers*

National Corrections and Law Enforcement
Training and Technology Center
West Virginia High-Technology
Consortium Foundation
$986,643
2005–DD–BX–K187

National Law Enforcement and Corrections
Technology Center
Aspen Systems Corporation
$2,884,930
2005–MU–CX–K077

National Law Enforcement and Corrections
Technology Center—Rocky Mountain Region
University of Denver—Colorado Seminary
$2,709,930
2005–IJ–CX–K001

National Law Enforcement and Corrections
Technology Center—Southeast Region
South Carolina Research Authority
$2,859,930
2002–MU–MU–K011

National Law Enforcement and Corrections
Technology Center—Western Region
Aerospace Corporation
$2,884,930
2005–IJ–CX–K030

Office of Law Enforcement Technology
Commercialization
West Virginia High-Technology
Consortium Foundation
$2,712,601
2005–IJ–CX–K003

Rural Law Enforcement Technology Center
Eastern Kentucky University
$2,859,930
2001–MU–MU–K009

Rural Law Enforcement Technology Center
Hazard, City of
$1,236,847
2005–DD–BX–0101

Southwest Public Safety Technology Center
University of Houston
$2,959,929
2003–IJ–CX–K011

TERRORISM AND CRITICAL
INCIDENTS

Building and Analyzing a Comprehensive
Open Source Database on Global Terrorist
Events, 1968–2005
University of Maryland
$106,702
2005–IJ–CX–0002

Geospatial Analysis of Terrorist Activities:
Patterns of Preparatory Behavior of
International and Environmental Terrorists
University of Arkansas
$314,840
2005–IJ–CX–0200

Kentucky Community Critical Infrastructure
Protection Laboratory
Eastern Kentucky University
$10,900,000
2004–IJ–CX–K055

National Bomb Squad Commanders
Advisory Board
National Law Enforcement and Corrections
Technology Center—Rocky Mountain
Center Operations
University of Denver—Colorado Seminary
$24,752
2005–IJ–CX–K107

Precision Indoor/Outdoor Personnel Location System, III
Worcester Polytechnic Institute
$1,973,286
2003–IJ–CX–K025

Strategies for Securing Subway and Rail Systems
RAND Corporation
$298,900
2005–IJ–CX–0059

Technologies for Public Safety in Critical Incident Response: NIJ National Conference and Exposition
Center for Technology Commercialization
$550,000
2001–LT–BX–K011

VICTIMIZATION AND VICTIM SERVICES

Assessing the Extent of Human Trafficking: A Community Outreach Approach
Vera Institute of Justice
$336,177
2005–IJ–CX–0053

Understanding and Improving Law Enforcement Responses to Human Trafficking
Northeastern University
$350,994
2005–IJ–CX–0045

Victims No Longer: Research on Child Survivors of Trafficking for Sexual and Labor Exploitation
Georgetown University
$175,496
2005–IJ–CX–0051

VIOLENCE

Evaluation of the Chicago Project for Violence Prevention
Northwestern University
$999,662
2005–MU–MU–0033

Evaluation of the Milwaukee Homicide Review Commission
Harvard College
$219,813
2005–IJ–CX–0005

Violent Crime Trends in Appalachian Counties, 1977–96
University of Missouri—St. Louis
$35,000
2005–IJ–CX–0011

Firearms

Child-Safe Personalized Weapons: Smart Gun Project
New Jersey Institute of Technology
$986,643
2004–IJ–CX–0096

Sexual Assault

Commercial Sexual Exploitation of Children in New York City: Population Assessment and Project Evaluation
New York, City of
$500,000
2005–LX–FX–0001

Drug-Facilitated, Incapacitated, and Forcible Rape: A National Study of Prevalence and Case Characteristics Among College Students and Other Young Women
Medical University of South Carolina
$447,796
2005–WG–BX–0006

Evaluation of Gender Violence and Harassment Prevention Programs in Middle Schools
Caliber Associates, Inc.
$425,210
2005–WT–BX–0002

Systems Change Analysis of SANE (Sexual Assault Nurse Examiner) Programs
Michigan State University
$389,925
2005–WG–BX–0003

Violence Against Women and Family Violence

Bruising as a Forensic Marker of Physical Elder Abuse
University of California—Irvine
$375,655
2005–IJ–CX–0048

Consequences of Childhood Exposure to Intimate Partner Violence
University of Chicago
$20,000
2005–WG–BX–0001

Detecting, Addressing, and Preventing Elder Abuse in Residential Care Facilities
Texas A&M Research Foundation
$208,354
2005–IJ–CX–0054

Elder Abuse: How Protective Behaviors and Risk Factors Affect the Course of Abuse Over Time
Police Foundation
$438,054
2005–WG–BX–0012

Evaluation of California's Batterer
Intervention Systems
Judicial Council of California
$250,902
2005-WG-BX-0004

Evaluation of the Rural Domestic Violence
and Child Victimization Enforcement Grant
Program Special Initiative: Faith-Based and
Community Organization Pilot Program
Advocates for Human Potential
$797,094
2005-IJ-CX-0050

Evaluation (Year Six) of a Multisite
Demonstration of Collaborations to Address
Domestic Violence and Child Maltreatment
Caliber Associates, Inc.
$300,000
2000-MU-MU-0014

Florida Elder Abuse Survey
University of South Florida
$235,585
2005-MU-MU-0052

In and Out of Harm's Way: Intimate Partner
Violence Among Women Over the Life Course
University of Minnesota
$20,000
2005-WG-BX-0002

Intimate Partner Violence: Effectiveness of
Councils in Producing Systems Change
University of Illinois—Urbana-Champaign
$356,830
2005-WG-BX-0005

Investigative Strategies for the Successful
Prosecution of Intimate Partner Violence
University of Alaska
$180,042
2005-WG-BX-0011

Justice System Responses to Intimate Partner
Violence in Asian Communities
University of Michigan
$570,448
2005-WG-BX-0009

Protective Order Violation Consequences,
Responses, and Costs: A Rural and Urban
Multiple Perspective Study
University of Kentucky
$650,022
2005-WG-BX-0008

Stalking Victim's Journey: Offender Patterns,
Victim Help-Seeking, and the Criminal
Justice Response
Safe Horizon
$277,807
2005-WG-BX-0007

Use of Polygraphs to Combat Violence
Against Women
BOTEC Analysis Corporation
$324,877
2005-WG-BX-0010

YOUTH

AMBERVIEW: Digitally Recording and
Storing 3-D Facial Images and Fingerprints
of School-Age Children
West Virginia High-Technology
Consortium Foundation
$986,643
2004-LT-BX-K002

Assessment of Minority Youth
Overrepresentation in the Alaska
Juvenile Justice System
University of Alaska
$143,926
2005-IJ-CX-0013

Crime During the Transition to Adulthood:
How Youth Fare as They Leave Out-of-
Home Care
University of Chicago
$259,782
2005-IJ-CX-0031

Evaluation of Utah's Youth and Families With
Promise Program
Justice Research and Statistics Association, Inc.
$994,613
2005-IJ-CX-0046

Event Dynamics and the Role of Third Parties
in Youth Violence
Temple University
$259,756
2005-IJ-CX-0036

Identifying and Managing Juvenile
Justice Delays
University of Chicago
$252,964
2005-IJ-CX-0041

Impact of Institutional Placement on the
Recidivism of Delinquent Youth
New York University
$20,000
2005-IJ-CX-0014

Past, Present, and Future of Juvenile Justice:
Assessing Policy Options
Urban Institute
$258,068
2005-IJ-CX-0039

W.E.B. Dubois Fellowship: The Impact of
Race, Structure, Discrimination, and
Culture on Youth Violence: A Multilevel
Longitudinal Investigation
University of Missouri—St. Louis
$75,237
2005-IJ-CX-0035

Appendix C
NIJ Publications, Products, and Web Dissemination in FY 2005

Most NIJ materials are free and can be obtained from these three sources:

- NIJ Web site: www.ojp.usdoj.gov/nij.

- National Criminal Justice Reference Service (NCJRS): www.ncjrs.gov, 800–851–3420, P.O. Box 6000, Rockville, MD 20849–6000.

- National Law Enforcement and Corrections Technology Center (NLECTC) (for science and technology materials): www.justnet.org, 800–248–2742.

CORRECTIONS

American Indian Suicides in Jail: Can Risk Screening Be Culturally Sensitive? Severson, Margaret, and Christine W. Duclos, Research for Practice, June 2005, 12 pages, NCJ 207326.

Drug Detection in Prison Mailrooms, In Short, November 2004, 3 pages, NCJ 205685.

"Reentry Programs for Women Inmates," *NIJ Journal,* No. 252, July 2005: 2–7.

"Special Technologies for Law Enforcement and Corrections," Falcon, William, *NIJ Journal,* No. 252, July 2005: 22–27.

Stress Among Probation and Parole Officers and What Can Be Done About It, Research for Practice, June 2005, 13 pages, NCJ 205620.

COURTS AND PROSECUTION

"Prosecutors' Programs Ease Victims' Anxieties," Chaiken, Marcia R., Barbara Boland, Michael D. Maltz, Susan Martin, and Joseph Tragonski, *NIJ Journal,* No. 252, July 2005: 30–33.

"Truth in Sentencing and State Sentencing Practices," Rosich, Katherine J., and Kamala Mallik Kane, *NIJ Journal,* No. 252, July 2005: 18–21.

CRIME CONTROL

Mapping Crime: Understanding Hot Spots, Eck, John E., Spencer Chainey, James G. Cameron, Michael Leitner, and Ronald E. Wilson, Special Report, August 2005, 77 pages, NCJ 209393.

Reducing Gun Violence: Operation Ceasefire in Los Angeles, Tita, George E., Jack Riley, Greg Ridgeway, and Peter W. Greenwood, Research Report, February 2005, 32 pages, NCJ 192378.

Reducing Gun Violence: The St. Louis Consent-to-Search Program, Decker, Scott H., and Richard Rosenfeld, Research Report, November 2004, 31 pages, NCJ 191332.

CYBER/ELECTRONIC CRIME

Test Results for Software Write Block Tools: PDBLOCK Version 1.02 (PDB_LITE), Special Report, June 2005, 37 pages, NCJ 209831.

Test Results for Software Write Block Tools: PDBLOCK Version 2.00, Special Report, June 2005, 88 pages, NCJ 209832.

Test Results for Software Write Block Tools: PDBLOCK Version 2.10, Special Report, June 2005, 93 pages, NCJ 209833.

FRAUD

"Telemarketing Predators: Finally, We've Got Their Number," *NIJ Journal,* No. 252, July 2005: 14–17.

HUMAN TRAFFICKING

"Tracking Modern Day Slavery," Bales, Kevin, *NIJ Journal,* No. 252, July 2005: 29–30.

INVESTIGATIVE AND FORENSIC SCIENCES

DNA in "Minor" Crimes Yields Major Benefits in Public Safety, In Short, November 2004, 2 pages, NCJ 207203.

Identifying Victims Using DNA: A Guide for Families, President's DNA Initiative, April 2005, 13 pages, NCJ 209493.

Mass Fatality Incidents: A Guide for Human Forensic Identification, Special Report, June 2005, 83 pages, NCJ 199758.

LESS-LETHAL TECHNOLOGIES

Department of Defense Nonlethal Weapons and Equipment Review: A Research Guide for Civil Law Enforcement and Corrections, Special Report, October 2004, 74 pages, NCJ 205293.

Impact Munitions Use: Types, Targets, Effects, Hubbs, Ken, and David Klinger, Research for Practice, October 2004, 16 pages, NCJ 206089.

POLICING

Calling 311: Guidelines for Policymakers, Mazerolle, Lorraine, Dennis Rogan, James Frank, Christine Famega, and John E. Eck, Research for Policy, February 2005, 7 pages, NCJ 206257.

Community Policing Beyond the Big Cities, Chaiken, Marcia R., Research for Policy, November 2004, 10 pages, NCJ 205946.

Español for Law Enforcement: An Interactive Training Tool, CD–ROM, February 2004, NCJ 201801.

Managing Calls to the Police With 911/311 Systems, Mazerolle, Lorraine, Dennis Rogan, James Frank, Christine Famega, and John E. Eck, Research for Practice, February 2005, 15 pages, NCJ 206256.

"The Voice Response Translator: A Valuable Police Tool," Cohen, Mark P., *NIJ Journal,* No. 252, July 2005: 8–13.

STANDARDS AND TESTING

Supplement I: Status Report to the Attorney General on Body Armor Safety Initiative Testing and Activities, Special Report, December 2004, 15 pages, NCJ 207605.

Third Status Report to the Attorney General on Body Armor Safety Initiative Testing and Activities, Special Report, August 2005, 47 pages, NCJ 210418.

TRANSNATIONAL CRIME

National Institute of Justice International Center: Building a Worldwide Criminal Justice Community, Program Brief (brochure), January 2005 [out of print].

"Tracking Modern Day Slavery," Bales, Kevin, *NIJ Journal,* No. 252, July 2005: 29–30.

VICTIMIZATION

"Prosecutors' Programs Ease Victims' Anxieties," Chaiken, Marcia R., Barbara Boland, Michael D. Maltz, Susan Martin, and Joseph Tragonski, *NIJ Journal,* No. 252, July 2005: 30–33.

"Tracking Modern Day Slavery," Bales, Kevin, *NIJ Journal,* No. 252, July 2005: 29–30.

Violence Against Women: Identifying Risk Factors, Research in Brief, November 2004, 16 pages, NCJ 197019.

VIOLENCE AGAINST WOMEN

Compendium of Research on Violence Against Women, 1993–2005, Rosen, Leora N., and Jocelyn Fontaine, eds., 158 pages at January 31, 2006 update, available at www.ojp.usdoj.gov/nij/vawprog/vaw_portfolio.pdf.

"The Decline of Intimate Partner Homicide," Wells, William, and William DeLeon-Granados, *NIJ Journal,* No. 252, July 2005: 33–34.

Violence Against Women: Identifying Risk Factors, Research in Brief, November 2004, 16 pages, NCJ 197019.

VIOLENT CRIME

Reducing Gun Violence: Operation Ceasefire in Los Angeles, Tita, George E., Jack Riley, Greg Ridgeway, and Peter W. Greenwood, Research Report, February 2005, 32 pages, NCJ 192378.

Reducing Gun Violence: The St. Louis Consent-to-Search Program, Decker, Scott H., and Richard Rosenfeld, Research Report, November 2004, 31 pages, NCJ 191332.

YOUTH

Toward Safe and Orderly Schools—The National Study of Delinquency Prevention in Schools, Gottfredson, Gary D., Denise C. Gottfredson, Ellen R. Czeh, David Cantor, Scott B. Crosse, and Irene Hantman, Research in Brief, November 2004, 20 pages, NCJ 205005.

NIJ JOURNAL

NIJ Journal, No. 252, July 2005, 34 pages, NCJ 208702.

ANNUAL REPORTS

NIJ 2004 Annual Report, National Institute of Justice, Annual Report to Congress, July 2005, 60 pages, NCJ 209274.

Exhibit C-1: Top 25 Publications Accessed From the NIJ Web Site, FY 2005

Title and Author	URL	NCJ Number	Published
DNA in "Minor" Crimes Yields Major Benefits in Public Safety (In Short)	www.ncjrs.gov/pdffiles1/nij/207203.pdf	NCJ 207203	2004
Crime Scene Investigation: A Reference for Law Enforcement Training (Special Report), Technical Working Group on Crime Scene Investigation	www.ncjrs.gov/pdffiles1/nij/200160.pdf	NCJ 200160	2004
Department of Defense Nonlethal Weapons and Equipment Review: A Research Guide for Civil Law Enforcement and Corrections (Special Report), National Security Research, Inc.	www.ncjrs.gov/pdffiles1/nij/205293.pdf	NCJ 205293	2004
Electronic Crime Scene Investigation: A Guide for First Responders (NIJ Guide), Technical Working Group on Crime Scene Investigation	www.ncjrs.gov/pdffiles1/nij/187736.pdf	NCJ 187736	2001
Crime Scene Investigation: A Guide for Law Enforcement (Research Report), Technical Working Group on Crime Scene Investigation	www.ncjrs.gov/pdffiles1/nij/178280.pdf	NCJ 178280	2000
Education and Training in Forensic Science: A Guide for Forensic Science Laboratories, Educational Institutions, and Students (Special Report), Technical Working Group for Education and Training in Forensic Science	www.ncjrs.gov/pdffiles1/nij/203099.pdf	NCJ 203099	2004
Violence Against Women: Identifying Risk Factors (Research in Brief)	www.ncjrs.gov/pdffiles1/nij/197019.pdf	NCJ 197019	2004
Death Investigation: A Guide for the Scene Investigator (Research Report), National Medicolegal Review Panel, and Steven C. Clark	www.ncjrs.gov/pdffiles/167568.pdf	NCJ 167568	1999
A Resource for Evaluating Child Advocacy Centers (Special Report), Shelly L. Jackson	www.ncjrs.gov/pdffiles1/192825.pdf	NCJ 192825	2004
Using DNA to Solve Cold Cases (Special Report)	www.ncjrs.gov/pdffiles1/nij/194197.pdf	NCJ 194197	2002
Guide for the Selection of Personal Protective Equipment for Emergency First Responders, 102-00, Vol. I (NIJ Guide), Alim A. Fatah, John A. Barrett, Richard D. Arcilesi, Jr., Charlotte H. Lattin, Charles G. Janney, and Edward A. Blackman	www.ncjrs.gov/pdffiles1/nij/191518.pdf	NCJ 191518	2002
The Sexual Victimization of College Women (Research Report), Bonnie S. Fisher, Francis T. Cullen, and Michael G. Turner	www.ncjrs.gov/pdffiles1/nij/182369.pdf	NCJ 182369	2000
Responding to Gangs: Evaluation and Research (Research Report), Winifred L. Reed and Scott H. Decker, eds.	www.ncjrs.gov/pdffiles1/nij/190351.pdf	NCJ 190351	2002
When Violence Hits Home: How Economics and Neighborhood Play a Role (Research in Brief), Michael L. Benson and Greer Litton Foxs	www.ncjrs.gov/pdffiles1/nij/205004.pdf	NCJ 205004	2004
Extent, Nature, and Consequences of Intimate Partner Violence: Findings From the National Violence Against Women Survey (Research Report), Patricia Tjaden and Nancy Thoennes	www.ncjrs.gov/pdffiles1/nij/181867.pdf	NCJ 181867	2000
Identifying Victims Using DNA: A Guide for Families (Brochure), President's DNA Initiative	www.ncjrs.gov/pdffiles1/nij/209493.pdf	NCJ 209493	2005
Toward Safe and Orderly Schools—The National Study of Delinquency Prevention in Schools (Research in Brief), Gary D. Gottfredson, Denise C. Gottfredson, Ellen R. Czeh, David Cantor, Scott B. Crosse, and Irene Hantman	www.ncjrs.gov/pdffiles1/nij/205005.pdf	NCJ 205005	2004
Arrestee Drug Abuse Monitoring: Annual Report, 2000 (Research Report)	www.ncjrs.gov/pdffiles1/nij/193013.pdf	NCJ 193013	2003
Stress Among Probation and Parole Officers and What Can Be Done About It (Research for Practice), Peter Finn and Sarah Kuck	www.ncjrs.gov/pdffiles1/nij/205620.pdf	NCJ 205620	2005
Mapping Crime: Understanding Hot Spots (Special Report), John E. Eck, Spencer Chainey, James G. Cameron, Michael Leitner, and Ronald E. Wilson	www.ncjrs.gov/pdffiles1/nij/209393.pdf	NCJ 209393	2005
Addressing Correctional Officer Stress: Programs and Strategies (Issues and Practices), Peter Finn	www.ncjrs.gov/pdffiles1/nij/183474.pdf	NCJ 183474	2000
Guide for the Selection of Chemical Agent and Toxic Industrial Material Detection Equipment for Emergency First Responders, 100-00, Vol. I (NIJ Guide), Alim A. Fatah, Richard D. Arcilesi, Jr., Kenneth J. Ewing, Charlotte H. Lattin, and Michael S. Helinski	www.ncjrs.gov/pdffiles1/nij/184449.pdf	NCJ 184449	2000
Reducing Gun Violence: The Boston Gun Project's Operation Ceasefire (Research Report), David M. Kennedy, Anthony A. Braga, Anne M. Piehl, and Elin J. Waring	www.ncjrs.gov/pdffiles1/nij/188741.pdf	NCJ 188741	2001
Impact Munitions Use: Types, Targets, Effects (Research for Practice), Ken Hubbs	www.ncjrs.gov/pdffiles1/nij/206089.pdf	NCJ 206089	2004
Hiring and Keeping Police Officers (Research for Practice), Office of Community Oriented Policing Services, and Christopher S. Koper	www.ncjrs.gov/pdffiles1/nij/202289.pdf	NCJ 202289	2004

Exhibit C-2: Top 25 Publications by Number of Paper Copies Requested, FY 2005

Title and Author	Quantity	NCJ Number	Published
What Every Law Enforcement Officer Should Know About DNA Evidence (Brochure), NIJ and the National Commission on the Future of DNA Evidence	9,010	NCJ 204892	1999
Identifying Victims Using DNA: A Guide for Families (Brochure)	6,180	NCJ 209493	2005
Electronic Crime Scene Investigation: A Guide for First Responders (NIJ Guide), Technical Working Group on Crime Scene Investigation	5,042	NCJ 187736	2001
Crime Scene Investigation: A Guide for Law Enforcement (Research Report), Technical Working Group on Crime Scene Investigation	3,765	NCJ 178280	1999
Death Investigation: A Guide for the Scene Investigator (Research Report), National Medicolegal Review Panel, and Steven C. Clark	2,789	NCJ 167568	1999
Forensic Examination of Digital Evidence: A Guide for Law Enforcement (Special Report), National Institute of Standards and Technology	2,745	NCJ 199408	2004
Eyewitness Evidence: A Guide for Law Enforcement (Research Report), Technical Working Group for Eyewitness Evidence	1,927	NCJ 178240	1999
Crime Scene Investigation: A Reference for Law Enforcement Training (Special Report), Technical Working Group on Crime Scene Investigation	1,672	NCJ 200160	2004
Español for Law Enforcement: An Interactive Training Tool (CD-ROM), Eastern Kentucky University Training Resource Center	1,663	NCJ 201801	2004
Emergency Responder Chemical and Biological Equipment Guides and Database (CD-ROM)	1,427	NCJ 197978	2003
Guide for Explosion and Bombing Scene Investigation (Research Report)	1,371	NCJ 181869	2000
Understanding DNA Evidence: A Guide for Victim Service Providers (Brochure), Kathryn M. Turman	1,365	NCJ 185690	2001
Fire and Arson Scene Evidence: A Guide for Public Safety Personnel (Research Report), Brian M. Dixon and Ronald L. Kelly, eds.	1,351	NCJ 181584	2000
Using DNA to Solve Cold Cases (Special Report)	1,321	NCJ 194197	2002
DNA in "Minor" Crimes Yields Major Benefits in Public Safety (In Short)	1,267	NCJ 207203	2004
Conflict Resolution for School Personnel, Materials Communication and Computer, Inc.	1,244	NCJ 194198	2002
What Every Law Enforcement Officer Should Know About DNA Evidence: Beginning Module #1 (CD-ROM), National Commission on the Future of DNA Evidence	1,200	NCJ 182992	2000
Mass Fatality Incidents: A Guide for Human Forensic Identification (Special Report), NIJ, the National Center for Forensic Science, and the Technical Working Group for Mass Fatality Forensic Identification	1,147	NCJ 199758	2005
What Every Law Enforcement Officer Should Know About DNA Evidence, Advanced Module #2 (CD-ROM), National Commission on the Future of DNA Evidence	1,103	NCJ 184479	2000
Evaluating G.R.E.A.T.: A School-Based Gang Prevention Program (Research for Policy), Finn-Aage Esbensen	1,089	NCJ 198604	2004
Advancing Justice Through DNA Technology (online document), U.S. Executive Office of the President	937	NCJ 200005	2003
NIJ Journal, Issue No. 251	914	NCJ 204515	2004
Reducing Gun Violence: The St. Louis Consent-to-Search Program (Research Report), Scott H. Decker and Richard Rosenfeld	889	NCJ 191332	2004
Eyewitness Evidence: A Trainer's Manual for Law Enforcement (Manual and CD-ROM), Technical Working Group for Eyewitness Evidence	870	NCJ 188678	2003
Violence Against Women: Identifying Risk Factors (Research in Brief)	854	NCJ 197019	2004

Exhibit C-3: NIJ Web Site Visits, FY 2003–2005

	FY 2003	FY 2004	FY 2005
NIJ Web Site	904,969	1,017,169	1,181,936
NIJ-Sponsored Sites*	**	959,473	1,294,898
Totals	904,969	1,976,642	2,476,834

*NIJ-sponsored Web sites include JUSTNET, which accounted for 1.2 million visits in FY 2005. (See chapter 6 for a description of JUSTNET.)

**Data not available.

The National Institute of Justice is the research, development, and evaluation agency of the U.S. Department of Justice. NIJ provides objective, independent, evidence-based knowledge and tools to enhance the administration of justice and public safety.

The National Institute of Justice is a component of the Office of Justice Programs, which also includes the Bureau of Justice Assistance, the Bureau of Justice Statistics, the Office of Juvenile Justice and Delinquency Prevention, and the Office for Victims of Crime.

Photo Sources: Getty Images, PunchStock, and Veer

NCJ 213267

www.ingramcontent.com/pod-product-compliance
Lightning Source LLC
Chambersburg PA
CBHW081841170526
45167CB00007B/2866